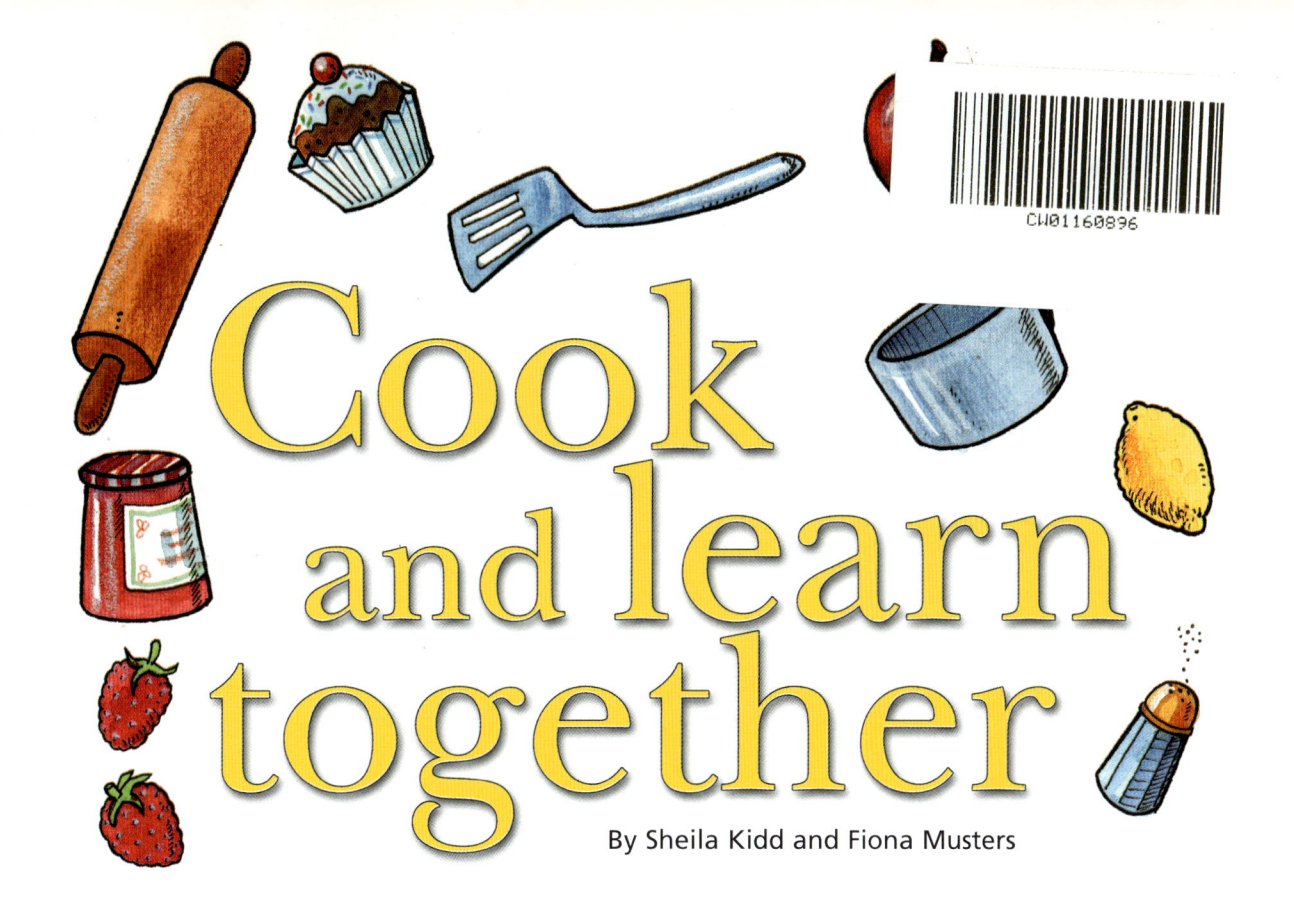

# Cook and learn together

By Sheila Kidd and Fiona Musters

### Soups
| | |
|---|---|
| Vegetable soup | 6 |
| Tomato soup | 9 |
| Mushroom soup | 11 |

### Salads, snacks and vegetables
| | |
|---|---|
| Egg, tomato and olive salad | 14 |
| Celery and apple salad | 14 |
| Avocado, orange and mozzarella salad | 15 |
| Carrot, orange and raisin salad | 17 |
| Panzanella | 19 |
| Potato salad | 21 |
| Cracked wheat salad | 23 |
| Vegetable curry | 25 |
| Tortilla | 28 |
| Crudites and cheese dip | 30 |

### Breads
| | |
|---|---|
| Basic bread | 34 |
| Focaccia | 38 |
| Pitta bread | 39 |
| Pizza | 41 |
| Hot cross buns | 43 |

### Pastry
| | |
|---|---|
| Little savoury tarts | 46 |
| Eccles cakes | 49 |
| Flaky mushroom tarts | 52 |
| Fish parcels | 54 |
| Sausage/cheesy rolls | 57 |
| Sausage plait | 59 |
| Sausage, tomato and onion pie | 61 |

### Puddings
| | |
|---|---|
| Jelly with fruit | 64 |
| Fruit salad | 66 |
| Apple charlotte | 68 |
| Pancakes | 70 |

### Cakes and biscuits
| | |
|---|---|
| Chocolate biscuit cake | 74 |
| Birthday cake | 76 |
| Flapjacks | 79 |
| Cheese biscuits | 81 |
| Shortbread biscuits | 83 |
| Gingerbread men | 85 |
| Fairy cakes | 88 |
| Mini Christmas cakes | 90 |

### No cook recipes
| | |
|---|---|
| Hummus bi tahini | 93 |
| Marzipan sweets | 95 |
| Chocolate fruit and nut clusters | 97 |

**How cooking helps children learn** 99

**Health and safety** 111

Illustrations and cover: Chantal Keys
Food styling: Liz Franklin
Photography: Roddy Paine

Published by Step Forward Publishing Limited
25 Cross Street, Leamington Spa, CV32 4PX
Tel: 01926 420046
www.practicalpreschool.com
© Step Forward Publishing Limited 2004

All rights reserved. No part of this publication may be reproduced, stored in a retrieval system, or transmitted by any means, electronic, mechanical, photocopied or otherwise, without the prior permission of the publisher.
Cook and learn together
ISBN: 1 904575 00 5

Cooking with young children should be fun but it's also a great way for them to learn. The food that you make together can be simple or complicated – the important thing is that you share an interest in all kinds of food.

Many children already cook at home, others have never had the chance to mix and stir, to get their hands onto a piece of dough or lick out the bowl of a pudding mix. It is surprising how capable many young children are. Some of them will be able to handle suitable knives, graters and whisks. Most will be enthusiastic about making pastry, kneading bread dough and spreading toppings on pizzas. Behind the fun, there is a serious message – that they can enjoy food that is tasty, nourishing and healthy.

## About this book

This book contains 40 recipes for children and adults to cook together as well as guidance on how cooking can help children learn. For professionals, we show how the activities fit in with the early years curriculum.

There is advice on storing food safely and tips on good practice when cooking with young children. We also give guidance on foods which may not be acceptable for medical or religious reasons. These are things you need to check if you're cooking with friends' children or children who are new to you.

## Recipes

The recipes are organised into chapters – soups, breads, pastry, for example. There are also a number of no-cook recipes.

Each recipe has:

- ingredients
- equipment
- how long it will take to prepare and cook
- what to do
- words you can use
- learning points
- related activities
- ways to check what children have learned

The activities can be adapted to suit the age of your children and to fit the time you have available.

## Ingredients

The recipes have been tried and tested using the amounts shown, but there may be times when you want to substitute one ingredient for another. Margarine can be used instead of butter without making too much difference. Smaller ingredients which add texture and interest can be swapped easily, either for your convenience or to suit children's tastes. Recipes containing nuts must be adapted for people with a nut allergy.

## Early learning

In England, the Early Learning Goals set out what most children should be able to do by the end of the Foundation Stage of education.

They cover six areas of learning: Personal, Social and Emotional Development; Communication, Language and Literacy; Mathematical Development; Knowledge and Understanding of the World; Physical Development and Creative Development.

The Foundation Stage runs from when a child is three to the end of their first year of compulsory schooling (Reception class). Don't expect your child to be achieving these goals when they are still in pre-school, aged three or four, as they will still be working towards them.

## Across the UK

There are different guidelines for pre-school education in Wales, Scotland and Northern Ireland but they have many similarities. They may use different words or the same words in a different order – but the expectations are essentially the same.

## Equipment

We provide a basic utensils list as well as some advice about electrical equipment. You should be able to make all the recipes with the equipment you have to hand in your kitchen at home. There are even some recipes that don't need an oven.

We list what you will need for each recipe but don't forget that if you do not have a particular utensil you may be able to improvise. If you don't have any pastry cutters, for example, the rim of a mug or cup will do the same job. A milk bottle makes a good rolling pin.

## Timing

The preparation time is a rough guide. Obviously, the more time you take with children to ask and answer questions, to notice changes, to find similarities and differences, the more time you will need.

Your children will want to see the result of their work and be eager to eat and share the food with friends or family, but try not to hurry so much that all the learning potential is lost.

Allow enough time to complete the tasks and remember, most learning happens during the process of cooking not eating!

## Words you can use

Each recipe has a short list of words you can use to expand children's vocabulary. Occasionally, the words are linked to a scientific concept and so should not be altered. For example, melt and dissolve are two distinct processes and the words should be used accurately.

## Learning points

Learning points tell you what to draw to children's attention and what kinds of questions to ask.

## Linked activities

These are ideas for activities that are connected in some way with ingredients in the recipe. They could be used while you are waiting for the food to cook or as follow-up activities later in the day or week.

Practical activities will help to broaden or deepen learning that has taken place during the cookery session. So, having looked at the oats used to make flapjacks, for example, you could show children that flour can be made from oats by grinding them in a make-shift pestle and mortar.

## What have children learned?

Each recipe includes some pointers in the form of questions to answer or signs to look for if you want to check what children have learned. Some points focus on older or more able children, recognising that children do not learn or develop at the same rate.

## TEACHING POINTS

### The early years curriculum

Most of the recipes will help children to meet the same learning outcomes but there are some which have the potential for promoting a particular aspect of learning, for example melting the chocolate for the chocolate biscuit cake or looking at circles when cutting out Eccles cakes. The outcomes listed are the most significant and obvious ones for each recipe.

### Personal, Social and Emotional Development

Every recipe will promote personal, social and emotional development - children will be trying new activities, concentrating, taking turns and learning to respect their own and other cultures. These outcomes are not listed.

### Involving parents

Make time to listen to parents as they talk to you about their child's attitudes to food and eating. They may have special cultural or religious knowledge of food and cooking which could be used to enhance the richness of children's experiences. For example, a parent who can make chapattis would be able to show how breads come in many different forms.

# Equipment

## Basic equipment

This is all you need to cook the recipes in this book - and many more.

Flat baking sheet
Loaf tin
Bun tin
Cooling rack
Pastry brush
Rolling pin
Pastry cutters
Saucepans
Whisk – rotary, balloon or hand-held electric
Wooden spoons
Tablespoons, teaspoons, forks
Sharp knife for adult use
Suitable knives for children's use
Weighing scales (metric)
Mixing bowls (4 medium-sized, 1 large)
Measuring jug, preferably plastic
Sieve (or 4 medium-sized sieves)
Chopping board (or 4 small boards)
Tin opener

## Consumable materials

Plastic wrapping film
Paper cases for buns
Disposable all-purpose cloths
Mild disinfectant
Labels
Plastic bags with ties
Foil containers
Aluminium foil

## Electrical equipment

A microwave can help to speed up the cooking and can be an advantage when time is short but unless you have a sophisticated model, cakes and biscuits can be pale and uninteresting and cheese can become stringy and tough.

A handmixer can be an advantage when whipping or mixing ingredients together. Changes can be faster, and so more fascinating.

## Small hand equipment

If you need to get any new equipment, think about buying enough for a small group of children to be as active and independent as possible. For instance, buy four small bowls and four mixing spoons, four rolling pins and plenty of extra and different sized spoons, forks and knives.

Mini kitchens on wheels can be a useful, if more expensive, buy for schools and nurseries. These portable units contain everything you need to get started.

Utensil boards are a good way of storing equipment. Utensils hang against a silhouette of their shape, making it easy to see when tools are missing and helping children to match when putting equipment back.

### TEACHING POINTS

If you provide meals to children, the chances are you will have a standard cooker. Mini cookers work well if space is restricted. They also have the advantage of being easy to transport if you buy one with a trolley.

An electric kettle will enable you to make jellies.

When you are setting up a cooking area there are a number of considerations: the space available, how much money you have and the range of cooking you will be doing.

If you have a freezing compartment in a fridge and a cooker with a hob and oven, there is virtually no limit to what you and the children can cook.

# Soups

If there is one thing that represents homeliness and comfort on a cold day it's soup. It is nourishing, satisfying and easy to digest. The three recipes in this chapter give many opportunities for children to compare vegetables of different shapes and sizes and to slice and chop to their hearts content.

# Vegetable soup

## Ingredients
Adapt to suit season and availability

2 large onions
2 large carrots
4 stalks of celery
2 cloves of garlic, crushed or finely chopped
6 tomatoes or a tin of Italian tomatoes
2 potatoes (or sweet potatoes)
3 courgettes
250g green beans trimmed into 3 cm lengths
1 tbsp tomato puree
1–1.5 litres Marigold vegetable stock or water
vegetable oil or olive oil
bunch of basil
grated Parmesan cheese
Other additions or substitutes could include sliced mushrooms, peas, broad beans, chopped cabbage or spinach

## Equipment
large saucepan
chopping board or suitable table
knives (sharp for adult, safe but able to cut for children)
vegetable peeler
spoons

**Preparation time:** 35 minutes

**Cooking time:** 20 minutes

This recipe gives you the chance to talk about all kinds of different vegetables, some of which can be sampled raw before they are made into soup. You will be able to talk about the differences in colour, shape, texture, smell and taste. A wonderful sensory experience lies ahead!

Take time to teach children how to use knives safely under close supervision. The knives should not, of course, be razor edged but they do need to be sharp enough to cut without pressing too hard.

### Method
Prepare the vegetables by peeling or scraping where necessary and show children that they need to wash vegetables if not peeling.

Plunge tomatoes in boiling water for 1 minute then into cold water and slip off the skins. Cut in half, remove the core and squeeze out most of the seeds, then chop into 1 cm pieces. Cut all the other vegetables (except beans) into similar sizes. It does not matter too much if there is some variation in size as it adds texture to the soup.

Place 30ml vegetable oil in a saucepan and heat. Put the onion in the pan and cook on a low heat until soft – about 3-5 minutes.

Add the potatoes, carrots and celery. Stir then add 1 litre water or stock, some seasoning and bring to simmer. Leave for 5–10 minutes, then add tomatoes, courgettes, beans and tomato puree. Simmer until beans are tender but still firm. Taste for seasoning and adjust.

Chop basil and mix into 2 tablespoons of olive oil. Put I teaspoon of this into each serving with some grated Parmesan.

### Action rhyme

Five little peas in a pea pod pressed
One grew, two grew and so did all the rest,
They grew and they grew and did not stop
Until one day the pod went pop!

To make a pea pod, hold the hands with palms flat together, gradually move the hands gently apart and end the rhyme with a clap.

## Learning points

**Words you can use**: names of vegetables and colours, peel, chop, slice

Take time to look closely at all the vegetables you are going to use. Talk about the different sizes, colours and shapes. Some vegetables grow under the ground, for example potatoes and carrots, others such as cabbage and spinach are leaves of plants, and courgettes and tomatoes contain the seeds of the plants. Celery is the stalk of a plant. Tell children that vegetables are good for us. They contain fibre and vitamins that help us to stay healthy.

Plunging tomatoes or fruit into boiling water is the standard way of removing the skin. Cut the tomato and look at the pattern of seeds inside.

Children will notice that some vegetables are more difficult to cut than others. Draw their attention to the different structures of the plants. For example, you may be able to see the small seeds in a courgette, or the stringy bits that run up a celery stalk. Talk about the shapes being made as you slice, for example, circles of carrot.

Encourage children to try some of the raw vegetables (not onions or potatoes!) Find out which they like best.

## Ideas for activities

- Read or tell the traditional tale 'The Giant Turnip' (Ladybird). The characters in this story all work together to pull up a giant turnip which they later cook, in some versions, into soup.

- Make a picture of all the characters in 'The Giant Turnip' pulling up the turnip.

- Are there any allotments or the garden of a keen vegetable grower you could visit? Many children do not recognise peas in the pod, brussel sprouts on the stalk or the feathery tops of carrot leaves.

- Take a trip to a greengrocer, market stall or a supermarket to look at fresh vegetables. This will be another chance to identify the vegetables you use in your soup as well as different shapes and sizes of the same vegetable. Are the vegetables displayed in a particular way, for example are all the salads together?

- Grow your own vegetables or herbs. If you have a patch of earth outdoors you can use, plant seeds that are easy to grow such as lettuce and radish.

- A sand tray or other container with deep sides makes an ideal mini-garden for indoors. Containers need lots of watering, and remember to make drainage holes in the base or plants will become

## TEACHING POINTS

**Communication, Language and Literacy**
Extend their vocabulary, exploring the meanings and sounds of new words

**Mathematical Development**
Use language such as 'circle' and 'bigger' to describe shape and size

**Knowledge and Understanding of the World**
Find out about and identify some features of living things they observe

**Physical Development**
Recognise the importance of keeping healthy and those things which contribute to this

Handle tools with increasing control

## Involving parents

Ask each child to bring a vegetable from home to use for growing. Carrot or parsnip tops will grow in a small dish of water placed in a sunny spot. A potato or old onion that has begun to sprout will continue to grow for a week or two without soil or water. Potatoes and onions will grow even faster in the dark.

waterlogged. Other suitable containers include yoghurt pots, foil food trays or large margarine or ice-cream cartons.

- Set up a greengrocer's stall to encourage imaginative play. Simple vegetables such as potatoes, carrots and cabbages can be made using a paper mache technique over scrunched-up newspaper and painted. Alternatively use real vegetables. They can always be turned into more soup when they begin to look a bit tired! You will need money, weighing scales and shopping bags and baskets.

- Have raw vegetables sometimes for a snack instead of biscuits. Carrots, celery sticks, slices of courgette and sweet red pepper are popular and go well with a simple cheese dip.

- Buy some of the cheaper vegetables for printing. Let the children cut the vegetables themselves. Make sure there is a variety of shapes - ovals from potatoes, circles, triangular shapes from carrots cut lengthwise. Cabbages and brussel sprouts make intriguing tree-like prints.

## TEACHING POINTS

### What have children learned?

Can children name all the vegetables and talk about their colour and shape?

Do they notice the different smells of the vegetables and show interest in tasting some of them?

Can they begin to cut some of the vegetables for themselves?

Are older children able to recognise that if they cut horizontally through a cylinder shape, for example a carrot, they will make a circle?

Are they able to name root vegetables such as turnips, parsnips and beetroot?

Are they able to notice small features of the vegetable they are slicing? Can they use words to describe these features?

Do they know that if they plant a tomato seed a new plant will grow?

COOK AND LEARN TOGETHER

# Easy tomato soup

**Ingredients**
60g butter
2 medium to large onions - finely chopped
2 sticks of celery, chopped
800g ripe tomatoes, cut into pieces by children
1 tsp sugar
800ml vegetable stock
130ml cream or rich milk
basil or parsley

**Equipment**
2-3 litre saucepan
knives
chopping board
blender, mouli or sieve

**Preparation time:**
25 minutes

**Cooking time** 20 minutes

There are many variations of this classic soup, but let's keep it simple. To avoid the need for peeling and deseeding the tomatoes, it's best to have a blender and/or mouli-legume. If you have neither of these a sieve will do but allow about 10 minutes extra at the end of the cooking time.

## Method
Slice the vegetables.

Melt the butter in a pan. Add the onion and celery, cook over a gentle heat, stirring occasionally, for about 15 minutes, adding a little water if necessary to prevent burning. Add the tomatoes, sugar and some salt and pepper. Stir and cook for 5 minutes.

Add the stock, bring to the boil and then simmer, covered, for 15 minutes or so.

Cool a little. Blend in a liquidiser if you have one or puree through a mouli to remove skin and seeds. You could use a sieve but it will take longer.

Reheat, adding chopped basil or parsley and cream.

## Learning points

**Words you can use:** slice, chop, seeds, skin, sieve, dissolve, liquidise

Slicing onions may make children's eyes water. The slicing releases a chemical that causes the crying. When you slice up the tomatoes, cut them in different ways so the pattern of seeds and flesh can be seen. Cut vertically from the stalk; on the next tomato slice across, then compare the patterns.

Sugar and salt may look the same but they taste different. Give children the chance to taste the difference.

Watch as the stock cube particles are dissolved in the boiling water. Then listen as the stock is added to the vegetables. Does it make a distinctive sound?

If you are using a sieve, children will be able to see the flesh and juice of the tomatoes dropping into the bowl while the skins and seeds are left behind. Ask children why the seeds and skins won't go through the sieve.

When you add the cream, make a swirl so children can see the contrasting colour and the pattern.

## Ideas for activities

- Place a variety of sieves, including a tea strainer and a colander, in some sand along with some small gravel stones so children can practise sieving.

- As the white cream is added to the tomato soup there is a slight change in colour. This can be copied using paint. Use ready-mixed paint; place a small amount of paint into an old margarine tub then swirl some white paint into the tub. See how red is changed to pink and dark blue to pale blue.

## TEACHING POINTS

**Communication, Language and Literacy**
Use talk to organise, sequence and clarify thinking, ideas, feelings and events

Extend their vocabulary

**Knowledge and Understanding of the World**
Look closely at similarities and differences, patterns and change

Ask questions about why things happen and how things work

### What have children learned?

Do children show an interest in the patterns inside tomatoes?

Can they tell salt from sugar?

Do they use the word 'dissolve' when water is added to the stock particles?

Can they explain why the seeds and skin don't pass through the sieve?

### Involving parents

Tell parents that their children have been practising sieving. Encourage them to sort out strainers and sieves at home for their children to play with in the bath.

# Mushroom soup

### Ingredients
500g mushrooms (a mixture, if possible, of flat, closed cup and chestnut)
1 small onion, chopped
2 cloves of garlic, finely chopped
800ml water
1 tsp Marigold vegetable stock powder
salt and pepper
30g butter
1tbsp cornflour mixed to a smooth paste with a little water
1 tbsp tomato puree
125ml double cream
2 tbsp chopped parsley

### Equipment
saucepan with lid
chopping board
knives
liquidiser (optional)

### Preparation time:
20 minutes

**Cooking time:** 30 minutes

**Most large supermarkets sell a range of mushrooms of different types and sizes. This not only adds interest to the preparation but flavour to the soup.**

### Method
Wash and cut the mushrooms into the smallest possible pieces.

Chop the onion and place in a pan of melted butter over a gentle heat. Stir gently for 3-4 minutes

Add the chopped mushrooms and garlic, mix well, then put the lid on the pan and sweat them over a very gentle heat for a further 3 to 4 minutes.

Carefully remove the lid, stir in the stock powder, tomato puree and water. Bring to the boil, turn heat to low and simmer with the lid on for about 20 minutes.

Add the cornflour mixture, stirring all the time, and simmer for a couple of minutes.

Season with salt and pepper to taste, add cream and parsley. Serve or cool.

For a smoother texture, puree the mixture in a liquidiser when cool, then reheat. Add cream and parsley.

## Learning points

**Words you can use**: mushrooms, fungus, gills, slice, liquidise

Look at the dark gills on the underside of the mushrooms (more obvious in flat mushrooms.) This is where the spores are made that produce new mushrooms.

Slicing onions may make children's eyes water. The slicing releases a chemical that irritates the eyes.

Let children observe the thickening process when the cornflour mixture is added.

## Ideas for activities

- Find a spare onion to show children how it will begin to grow. Place it in a dish of water (not too much or the bulb will rot). Keep it for a week or so and the roots will begin to grow and the centre should show signs of stem growth.

- Mushrooms are fungi and produce spores, not seeds. To see the microscopic spores take an almost open mushroom and place it on a piece of clean white paper. In a few days, when the gills open, the spores will be released and fall onto the paper to create a spore print.

### Safety note
Children may come across wild fungi that appear to them to be mushrooms. Although many wild fungi are edible there are some which are poisonous. Explain this to children and warn them not to eat mushrooms they see growing in the wild, just as you would warn them about eating wild berries.

## TEACHING POINTS

**Communication, Language and Literacy**

Use talk to organise, sequence and clarify thinking, ideas, feelings and events

Extend their vocabulary

**Knowledge and Understanding of the World**

Look closely at similarities and differences, patterns and change

Ask questions about why things happen and how things work

### What have children learned?

Do children show an interest and curiosity in the structure of the mushrooms?

Are they able to identify times when they have cried?

Do they notice the changes in the soup after it has been liquidised?

# Salads, snacks and vegetables

Many of the recipes in this chapter do not need cooking but are included because they contain vegetables. For a healthy lifestyle we need to eat plenty of fruit and vegetables which are naturally high in dietary fibre and vitamins, especially when eaten raw. Many vegetables are quick to prepare and make ideal snacks.

As we rely more and more on processed food many children are becoming less familiar with vegetables in their natural state, for example peas and broad beans in their pods or carrots with their feathery leaved tops. These recipes give you the chance to explore their different colours, smells, textures and tastes.

# Simple salads

**Ingredients**
hard-boiled egg quarters
cherry tomatoes
olives

**Egg, tomato and olive salad**

## Method
Boil the eggs for ten minutes. Once they are boiled, cool them quickly in running cold water so that the yolks do not become discoloured with a grey ring.

Children will enjoy cracking the eggs and peeling off the shell. This is easily achieved under a little running water. Cherry tomatoes are readily available in supermarkets. Green or black olives may be bought fresh, bottled or canned: a mixture of olives would enable you to talk about the varying shapes, colours, sizes and flavours!

Mix all the ingredients together!

# Celery salad

**Ingredients**
2 sticks of celery
1-2 eating apples
cucumber (approximately 10 cm)
small carton of plain yoghurt
a few nuts and raisins

This makes a creamy salad. Celery and apple flavours complement one another and the nuts and raisins add textural interest. The amount of each ingredient is not precise.

## Method
Chop the celery, cucumber and apple. Mix with some nuts or raisins and stir into yoghurt.

# Avocado, orange and mozzarella salad

This salad won't take long to make. The main ingredients are served on the boat shaped leaves of little gem lettuce. This makes it easy to eat and children will enjoy preparing their own little portion.

## Method

Peel the avocados by cutting into quarters lengthwise, removing the stone and pulling off the skin. Cut into thin slices and sprinkle with lemon juice to prevent discolouring.

Peel the oranges, segment and remove any pips. Add to the bowl of avocado. Season with salt and pepper and mix in 2 tablespoons of olive oil and herbs.

Wash the lettuce and arrange the avocado mix on the top.

Slice the mozzarella and put on top, sprinkling with a little more seasoning and olive oil.

### Ingredients

2 ripe avocados
2 oranges
250g fresh mozzarella cheese
salt, pepper, virgin olive oil
juice of half a lemon
1 tsp chopped fresh thyme or basil (optional)
1 little gem lettuce, washed and dried

### Equipment

chopping board
knives
small mixing bowl
serving platter

**Time:** 15 minutes to assemble all the ingredients

## Learning points

**Words you can use**: stone, pips, segments, peel, slice

Many children will not have seen an avocado pear. It has a uniquely textured skin so let children feel it before starting the peeling. The stone is likely to be the largest seed they have seen in a fruit. Tell children that the lemon juice is to stop the pear from turning brown.

As you break the orange into segments, find the pips and compare them to the size of the avocado stone.

As you wash the lettuce, help children to notice the texture of the leaves. Little gem lettuces are renowned for their crinkly leaves.

Tell children that there are thousands of different cheeses. This one is called mozzarella and it comes from Italy.

## Ideas for activities

- Try some slithers of cheese for a snack so children experience some of the variety available. Pick mild cheeses such as Edam, mild cheddar, mozzarella.

### TEACHING POINTS

**Communication, Language and Literacy**
Use talk to organise, sequence and clarify thinking, ideas, feelings and events
Extend their vocabulary

**Knowledge and Understanding of the World**
Look closely at similarities and differences, patterns and change
Ask questions about why things happen and how things work

### What have children learned?

Do they use comparative language (bigger, smaller) when comparing the seeds from the avocado and the orange?

Do they notice the different textures? The leathery and bumpy skin of the avocado, the soft pith lining the orange skin and the crinkly leaves of the lettuce.

### Involving parents

Ask parents to help their children collect pips and stones from fruit. Summer is a good time to do this when peaches, plums and cherries are available as well as oranges, apples and pears. Once they have been admired for their similarities and differences they can be used in collage pictures.

COOK AND LEARN TOGETHER

# Carrot, orange and raisin salad

**Ingredients**
400g carrots
4 oranges
100g raisins
20ml virgin olive oil
salt and pepper
juice of half a lemon
2 tbsp chopped parsley (optional)

**Equipment**
chopping boards
mixing bowls
grater
peeler
knives

**Preparation time:**
20 minutes

This is an easy-to-follow recipe with a waiting time of 15 minutes to allow the flavours to mix and meld. The salad will be ready for eating as soon as the washing and tidying up has been done!

## Method

Peel and wash the carrots. Grate them, taking care no one scrapes or cuts their knuckles.

Peel the oranges and divide into segments, cutting each segment into 2 or 3 pieces.

Mix the raisins, carrot and orange together in a bowl, adding some salt and pepper and the lemon juice. Mix in the olive oil and parsley.

Leave to soften for 15 minutes. Adjust seasoning if necessary, maybe adding a little sugar.

### Nursery rhyme

**Oranges and lemons**
Oranges and lemons
Say the bells of St Clement's.

You owe me five farthings,
Say the bells of St Martin's.

When will you pay me?
Say the bells of Old Bailey.

When I grow rich,
Say the bells of Shoreditch.

Pray, when will that be?
Say the bells of Stepney.

I'm sure I don't know,
Says the great bell at Bow.

Here comes a candle to light you to bed,
And here comes a chopper to chop off your head!

## Learning points

**Words you can use**: grate, segments, soak

If you have a box grater there will be a range of grating sizes to choose from. Let children experiment and see the different sized pieces they can make. The best size is likely to be one in the middle range.

Help children to see that oranges have many wrappings: the outer waxy skin, the soft downy pith, and the membrane around each segment. Within each segment are hundreds of tear-shaped pieces of flesh. The pips are usually right at the centre. All these wrappings are to protect the pips which will grow into new plants.

Talk to children about all the different colours they can see.

Flavours are often better when they have had a little time to meld and blend together.

## Ideas for activities

- Play pass the parcel. Use about six different wrappings with a surprise in the centre. The parcel with its different layers of wrapping represents the orange with its many parts.

- Sing 'Oranges and lemons'.

- While you are waiting for the salad to be ready, ask children to find some objects which are orange, brown or green - the colours in the salad.

## TEACHING POINTS

**Communication, Language and Literacy**
Use talk to organise, sequence and clarify thinking, ideas, feelings and events

Extend their vocabulary

**Knowledge and Understanding of the World**
Look closely at similarities and differences, patterns and change

Ask questions about why things happen and how things work

## What have children learned?

When examining the parts of an orange, are children interested and do they talk about what they notice?

Are children able to name the following colours: orange, brown, and green?

## Involving parents

Ask parents to save a carrot top for their child to bring in. When carrot tops are set in a little dish of water the tops will begin to sprout into leaf.

COOK AND LEARN TOGETHER

# Panzanella

## Ingredients
3 thick slices of Italian style bread
25-50ml water or tomato juice
1 clove of garlic, crushed (optional)
2 or 3 ripe tomatoes, skinned and chopped
1 small red and 1 small yellow pepper
half a cucumber, peeled and chopped into 1cm dice
20 black olives, pitted (optional)
10 basil leaves, torn
2 tbsp virgin olive oil

## For dressing
2 tbsp virgin olive oil
1 tbsp balsamic vinegar
salt and pepper

## Equipment
knives for you and children
chopping board
serving bowl
spoon for mixing

**Preparation time:** allow anything from 25 to 40 minutes

The flavours will improve if the salad is left for 20 minutes before eating.

Here is another recipe for using up stale bread (good quality, country style bread not sliced). This salad can only be made in the summer when tomatoes are ripe and tasty. This is a simplified version for children of what is basically a traditional Italian peasant dish. It gives plenty of scope to talk about colours, textures and flavours.

## Method
Show children how to tear the bread into pieces, place in a bowl and moisten with the water or juice. Leave to soak for 15 minutes.

Chop the vegetables.

Squeeze and crumble the bread (some of the children will delight in getting their hands in) and pour on the olive oil.

Mix in the remaining ingredients, giving a good stir.

Mix the dressing ingredients together using the seasoning with discretion and pour over the salad.

## Learning points

**Words you can use:** tear, soak, squeeze, crumble

Children will enjoy tearing the bread. If it is stale (as it should be) it may be a little tough on their hands. They may notice that, as they tear, the air holes in the bread become squashed. As the liquid is poured over the bread, ask children where it goes. Do they realise that the bread has soaked it up?

Compare sizes, colours, smells and textures of the vegetables as they are sliced.

The children should notice a difference in the feel of the bread once it has been soaked.

When the vegetables are added there will be plenty of opportunity for stirring practice.

Oil does not mix readily with other liquids. Take time to watch what happens in the process of making the dressing. Can children see the dark vinegar lying underneath the oil? Swirl the ingredients gently to see how the vinegar gradually merges with the oil.

## Ideas for activities

- Tear bread for the birds, but only in the winter months. It is harmful for baby birds to be fed bread.

- Buy some cheap fresh bread to make bread sculptures. Bread is easily shaped when it's fresh, but white bread can turn grey when it is manipulated for too long! Finished sculptures can be left to dry and grow hard.

- Try mixing a number of liquids with a cheap vegetable oil. Do all liquids act the same way? Which look prettiest?

## TEACHING POINTS

**Communication, Language and Literacy**
Use talk to organise, sequence and clarify thinking, ideas, feelings and events

Extend their vocabulary

**Knowledge and Understanding of the World**
Look closely at similarities and differences, patterns and change

Ask questions about why things happen and how things work

**Physical Development**
Handle materials with increasing control

## What have children learned?

Are children able to use their hands well to tear, squeeze and crumble and stir the bread?

Do they compare colours, textures and sizes of vegetables when they are cutting and chopping?

## Involving parents

Ask parents if they have a lava lamp you could borrow so that children can see how heated oil moves.

# Potato salad

**Ingredients**
500g new potatoes
80ml bought or home-made mayonnaise
bunch of chives
spring onions
salt

**Optional extras:**
chopped hard-boiled egg
chopped walnuts
chopped parsley
50ml vinaigrette or french dressing

**Equipment**
saucepan
knives
bowl
vegetable brush
chopping board

**Time:** 30 minutes preparation and cooking, 5 minutes finishing

There are many variations on potato salad. This basic recipe is quick and easy and has a number of options to ring the changes. The ingredients are cheap and readily found in local stores.

## Method

Scrape or scrub the skins from the potatoes. Put them in a saucepan with cold water, add a level teaspoon of salt and bring to simmer covered for 15–20 minutes until tender.

Drain and cool until the potatoes can be handled. Let children chop them into 1 cm pieces and place in a bowl.

Trim, wash and chop the spring onions and chives and add to the bowl.

Add the mayonnaise and mix.

## Variations

Mix with vinaigrette and add chopped parsley and chives. Top with chopped hard-boiled egg.

## Learning points

**Words you can use**: scrub, skin, chop, mix, stir

Talk about the difference between new potatoes that only need to be scrubbed and old, which need to be peeled. Explain that some foods we can eat raw or cooked, for example carrots, but that raw potato is not nice or good for the stomach. We always have to cook potatoes before we eat them.

The potatoes may still be warm as children chop them up. Help them to notice the change. You might be able to see small amounts of steam rising from the potatoes as they are cut up. Talk about the shapes they can see as they are cutting.

## Ideas for activities

- Keep one potato on a windowsill and one in a dark cupboard and watch what happens over the next few weeks. (An old potato works best in the dark cupboard.) The children will be able to see the potato begin to sprout from the 'eyes'.

- Use potatoes for printing. Encourage children to cut their own potatoes so that the shapes are varied and interesting and they can develop their physical skills.

- Use potatoes as the base for making animals - real and imaginary. Any materials can be used - feathers, card - but cocktail sticks will be useful for making limbs.

## TEACHING POINTS

**Communication, Language and Literacy**
Use talk to organise, sequence and clarify thinking, ideas, feelings and events

Extend their vocabulary

**Knowledge and Understanding of the World**
Look closely at similarities and differences, patterns and change

Ask questions about why things happen and how things work

**Physical Development**
Handle tools with increasing control

### What have children learned?

Can they use the words 'warm', 'hot', 'cool' and 'cold' appropriately?

Can they talk about their favourite way of eating potatoes? (boiled, chipped, baked, mashed, roast)

Can they use the key words: scrub, skin, chop, mix, stir?

### Involving parents

Ask parents to help their children find some pictures of cooked potatoes in magazines. These can be used to help children make a tally of their favourite way of eating potatoes.

## Rhyme

One potato, two potato, three potato, four,
Five potato, six potato, seven potato more.

Children sit with both fists clenched in front of them. They recite the rhyme in time to the words, gently alternately striking one fist against another.

# Cracked wheat salad

**Ingredients**
150g cracked wheat
4 tomatoes
½ cucumber
bunch of flat-leafed parsley
bunch of spring onions
10 sprigs of fresh mint
½ bunch of coriander
juice of 2 lemons
80ml olive oil
salt and pepper
little gem lettuce leaves (optional)

**Equipment**
chopping board
mixing bowl
knives
fine sieve
teaspoon

**Preparation time:**
20 minutes

**Marinating time:**
15 minutes

**Assembly:** 5 minutes

There are many varieties of this Lebanese salad and you can adjust the ingredients to suit the children or availability. There will be plenty of opportunities for children to notice the fragrance of fresh herbs as they are chopped and to find the seeds in tomatoes, cucumber and lemon.

## Method

Soak the cracked wheat in enough cold water to cover and leave to stand for 15-20 minutes while you prepare the other ingredients.

Cut the cucumber and tomatoes in half lengthways and remove the seeds with a teaspoon. Cut in half again and let children chop them into small pieces.

Help them to pull the leaves off the parsley, coriander and mint stalks and chop them. Trim the spring onions and chop them into small pieces.

Drain the cracked wheat through a sieve, pressing well and tip into a bowl.

Mix the lemon juice with half the olive oil in a small bowl, then pour it onto the cracked wheat. Season with salt and pepper to taste and leave for 15 minutes or longer if convenient.

When ready to serve, stir in the herbs, onions, tomatoes and cucumber and mix well. Add more olive oil to taste, and serve with little gem lettuce leaves to scoop it with or a spoon and fork.

## Learning points

**Words you can use:** soak, absorb, smell, seeds, chop, leaves

When you leave the wheat to soak, draw children's attention to what it looks like in the bowl and tell them that it will change. What do they think will happen? It will appear that some of the water has disappeared but of course the wheat will have absorbed the water.

As you cut the tomatoes and cucumber in half children will be able to see the seeds and the centre. Help them to describe the size, colour and shape of the seeds. Although they are not needed in the recipe you could keep them and dry them for further investigation. If the lemon has a pip you can point out that the seeds of fruit, for example apples, oranges and pears, are called pips.

There will be plenty of opportunities for you to discuss the fragrances of the herbs as they are cut up.

When you return to the wheat, ask children if they notice that the pieces have become larger because they have absorbed the water. As you make the dressing, ask children to watch the olive oil carefully. It won't mix well with other ingredients unless it is stirred.

## Ideas for activities

- Using left-over herbs from this recipe or any others you may have readily available, play a blindfold game of identifying two or three herbs by smell.

- Find out what other foods will absorb water when they are soaked or cooked. Try butter beans, cous cous, butterfly pasta. Boiling water can speed up absorption.

- Make some marbled patterns by using cooking oil and a small amount of powder paint mixed together. Put small drops on the surface of a tray of water. Get children to notice how the oil mixture floats on the top of the water. Place a sheet of paper gently over the coloured oil and lift carefully. The oil will have stuck to the paper. Set aside to dry.

- Little gem lettuce leaves are boat shaped. Visit a greengrocer to make a collection of different shaped leaves. To cut costs, ask for some discarded leaves. Try cauliflowers, Savoy cabbage, carrots and curly kale. Point out that we eat leaves from some plants but not others.

## TEACHING POINTS

**Communication, Language and Literacy**
Use talk to organise, sequence and clarify thinking, ideas, feelings and events

Extend their vocabulary

**Knowledge and Understanding of the World**
Look closely at similarities and differences, patterns and change

Ask questions about why things happen and how things work

**Physical Development**
Handle tools with increasing control

### What have children learned?

Do children notice changes in the wheat? Can they begin to use the word 'absorb'?

Do they recognise that the cucumber and tomato have seeds? Do they know that if they plant seeds they will grow into new plants?

Can they distinguish the different fragrances of the herbs?

### Involving parents

Ask parents to save some of the seeds they find when they are preparing food. Make a seed collection and talk about different colours, sizes and shapes.

# Vegetable curry

**Ingredients for sauce**
2 onions, chopped
6 cloves of garlic, chopped
1-2 fresh red chillies, deseeded and finely chopped
1 lemon, zest for the sauce and juice for later
small bunch of fresh coriander
1/2 tsp curry powder
1/2 tsp turmeric
1 tsp ground cumin
3 tbsp vegetable oil

2 medium potatoes, peeled and cut into small chunks
1 medium aubergine cut into small cubes
200g butternut squash or other suitable squash – peeled and seeds removed, then chopped into cubes
150g mushrooms, chopped or sliced
400g can chopped tomatoes
250g green beans (runner or French) sliced
250ml coconut milk (from a tin)
350ml Marigold vegetable stock

1tbsp chopped fresh parsley or basil to finish

**Equipment**
chopping boards
knives
heavy gauge saucepan or frying pan
can opener
wooden spoon
teaspoon
blender if available

**Preparation time:**
30 minutes

**Cooking time:** 30 minutes

This is a dish that is open to many interpretations and can be varied according to the seasons. It is a good introduction for children who are not familiar with spicy foods because it is not too hot. It is suitable for vegetarians and may have other additions such as tofu or kidney beans.

**Warning:** Keep fresh chillies away from children and wash your hands thoroughly after handling them as they are an irritant.

## Method

Prepare the ingredients for the sauce, letting the children do as much of the cutting and chopping as they can with the exception of the chillies. If using a blender, place the ingredients for the sauce in it (apart from the oil), and blend to a puree. If you don't have a blender, chop everything as finely as possible.

Prepare the vegetables.

Heat the oil in a pan over a medium heat and add the mixture for the sauce. Stir and then turn the heat to low and cook for about 8 minutes.

Add the potatoes, squash, aubergine, tomatoes and stock, stir well and season with salt and pepper. Bring to the boil and then simmer for 10 minutes. Add the mushrooms and beans. Continue simmering until the beans are tender.

Add the coconut milk and cook for a few more minutes, then stir in the lemon juice and herbs. Serve with pitta or naan bread or rice (about 30g per child).

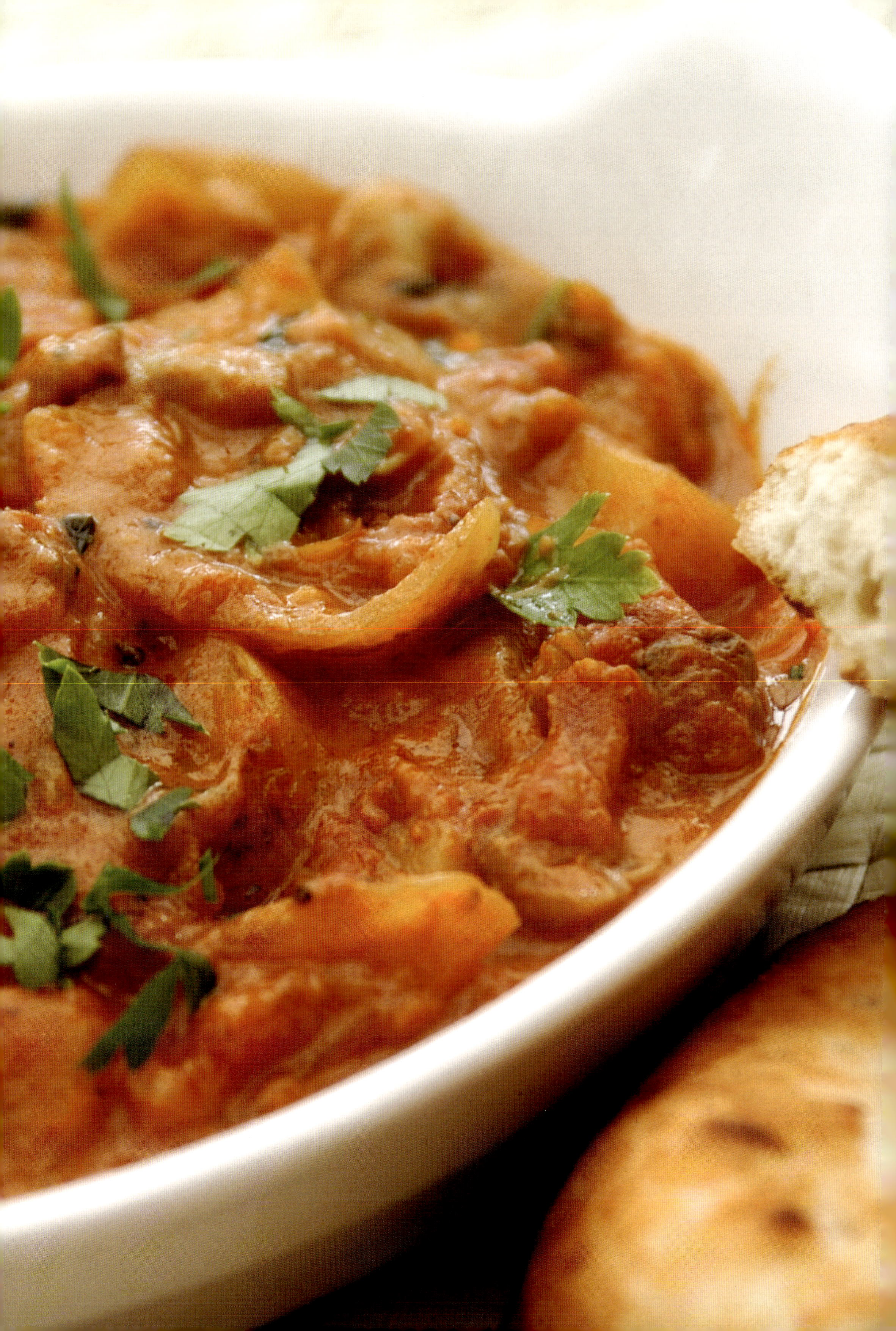

## Learning points

**Words you can use**: smell, spices

Most of the ingredients for the sauce have strong aromas so this is a good time for children to explore their sense of smell.

If you are using a blender, talk about how the blender works. Be sure to point out to children that they must not touch the sharp blades.

Look closely at the vegetables you are going to use. Talk about the different colours, sizes and shapes. Inside the aubergine, butternut squash and French beans you will see a variety of shapes and sizes of seeds.

When the spices are added to the warm pan, the aroma will become more pungent.

Listen out for the sound as the cold vegetables are added to the warm spices. Watch as the vegetables are coloured by the spice mixture.

## Ideas for activities

- Buy a whole coconut to cut open and feed to the birds. Ask children to feel the hairy outer skin. This hair is used to make coconut mats and peat free compost. Shake the coconut so that children hear the liquid inside. Notice the small indentations in the outer shell at the top. If you pierce or drill these holes you can place a long straw inside to drink the coconut milk. Alternatively, take the coconut outside and, keeping the children well back at a safe distance, use an axe to cut the coconut open. The milk will flow out.

- Coconut may be chipped out for the children to taste – give it a good wash first! Children may be familiar with coconut in its dessicated form. It is used in a popular chocolate bar, in sweets such as coconut ice and in cakes, biscuits and puddings.

- For more activities with vegetables, see page 7.

- Dry the butternut squash seeds and use them for a collage.

## TEACHING POINTS

**Communication, Language and Literacy**
Use talk to organise, sequence and clarify thinking, ideas, feelings and events
Extend their vocabulary

**Mathematical Development**
Use language to describe shape

**Knowledge and Understanding of the World**
Look closely at similarities and differences, patterns and change
Ask questions about why things happen and how things work

## What have children learned?

Can children name the vegetables and talk about their shape, colour, size?
Do they notice the smell of the spices?
Can they cut some of the vegetables for themselves?
Do they know that if they plant the seeds from the vegetables they could grow new plants?

## Involving parents

Ask parents to look out for products that contain coconut when they are shopping with their children.

# Tortilla

This classic Spanish snack is fun to make and can be eaten warm or at room temperature and is another good picnic food. If you do not have a large enough pan, make two tortillas in a smaller pan.

## Method

Encourage children to peel and chop the onion, although you may have to take over!

Place half the oil in a saucepan and soften the onion over a gentle heat for about 10 minutes. Remove from the heat and drain any excess oil into a frying pan.

Add butter to the oil in the frying pan and heat, tip in the potatoes and season with salt and pepper. Stir for a couple of minutes, making sure they do not brown. Then transfer them to a bowl.

Let children break the eggs into a cup, one at a time, adding each one to the bowl after making sure there is no shell in it.

Combine the egg mixture with the potatoes and onions and stir all of the ingredients, making sure everything is well mixed.

Now heat the rest of the oil in the frying pan and pour in the egg mixture, stirring with a wooden spoon until the mixture begins to set.

Let the tortilla colour underneath and then place the plate upside down on top of the pan. Holding the plate, turn the pan upside down so the tortilla is on the plate. Slide carefully back into the pan to finish cooking.

This can be eaten warm or left to cool for a snack or picnic.

**Ingredients**
1 large onion
300g new potatoes cooked in their skins, peeled whilst warm and chopped into 2cm chunks
50ml olive oil
20g butter
4 large eggs
salt and pepper

**Equipment**
gas or electric hob
small saucepan
large frying pan, preferably non-stick
chopping board
knives
whisk or fork
bowl
cup
large plate, about the same size as the frying pan

**Preparation time:**
10 minutes for cooking potatoes

**Cooking time:**
20 – 30 minutes

## Learning points

**Words you can use**: egg yolk, egg white, shell, skin, peel, chop, whisk, upside down

Children may find it difficult to peel an onion, as the papery skin can be slippery and sliced onion can make the eyes sting and water. Peeling an onion under a cold running tap can help. If you slice the onion around the centre you will see the concentric growth rings similar to those on a sliced tree trunk. If you slice the onion from top to bottom you will see a different pattern.

Point out that the onions gradually change from white to golden brown as they cook.

Explain that stirring the potatoes prevents them from burning.

Point out the different parts of an egg. As well as the yolk and the white, you might be able to see the air sac at the top of the egg inside the shell. Ask children to describe the changes in the eggs as they are whisked together.

It is important that all the egg is cooked before the tortilla is turned out ready for eating. Egg changes quickly as it is heated; from a liquid to a solid, binding together ingredients which are mixed with it. Do children notice how the onion and potato pieces are joined to the egg as it cooks?

Before you turn the tortilla onto a plate, tell children that you are going to turn it upside down and that the top side in the pan will become the bottom side on the plate.

## Ideas for activities

▪ Give children a small frying pan and plate and some coloured paper circles to play with. Make one side of the circles yellow and one side brown so that the children can clearly see what happens when they turn the tortillas out on the plate.

▪ Make up and tell the story of 'The runaway tortilla' in the same format as 'The gingerbread man'.

## TEACHING POINTS

**Communication, Language and Literacy**
Use talk to organise, sequence and clarify thinking, ideas, feelings and events
Extend their vocabulary

**Knowledge and Understanding of the World**
Look closely at similarities and differences, patterns and change
Ask questions about why things happen and how things work

**Physical Development**
Handle materials with increasing control

## What have children learned?
Can children see the different parts of the egg?
Can they predict what will happen to the egg as it is cooked?
Do they have enough physical control to break an egg?

## Involving parents
Tortillas make a simple and nourishing meal and can be easily adapted. Try any of the following; cook bacon bits with the onions, sprinkle in any left-over cold peas. When cold, spread with Marmite. Give a copy of the recipe to parents.

# Crudités with a cheese dip

**Ingredients for dip**
250g soft curd cheese
50g natural yoghurt
pinch of salt and paprika
25ml virgin olive oil
1 tbsp chopped parsley
clove of garlic, crushed
(optional)

**Ingredients for crudités**
2 carrots
3 sticks of celery
5 firm mushrooms
1 red or yellow pepper
cauliflower or broccoli florets
1 cucumber

**Equipment**
potato peeler
tablespoon
knives for children
forks
small bowl
chopping board

**Total time:** 20-30 minutes

Crudités are match-stick lengths of raw vegetables which can be eaten with a dip. A recipe is hardly needed for the crudités as you can use a selection of any vegetables that can be eaten raw. Those that are unsuitable include potato, aubergine, artichokes and onions. The cheese dip can be flavoured in many ways. This is a basic recipe that you can experiment with.

This is an easy to prepare recipe and makes an excellent light snack. It is also good for picnics.

## Method

Tip the cheese and yoghurt into a bowl. Add all the other dip ingredients and beat well with a fork. Taste and adjust seasoning if necessary. Keep cool.

Peel the carrots and wash all the vegetables. Cut and slice the vegetables into sticks suitable for dipping (about 4-5 cm x 1 cm).

## Learning points

**Words you can use**: cut, slice, mix, names of vegetables used

Watch what happens to the parsley as the dip mixture is stirred. Because it is green it is easily seen, but what about the salt? Is it still there even though you can't see it? How could you find out if it is there?

Examine the different vegetables before they are washed and sliced. Talk about the different textures and shapes: the ribbed celery, the shiny skin of a pepper, the tiny bobbles of a cauliflower floret. Compare the smells of the vegetables - are some stronger than others? They will smell more distinctive as they are sliced. Explore the colours and shades, for example celery is usually paler at the bottom of the plant.

We eat different parts of plants: usually the stalk of celery and sometimes the sweet leaves near the centre, the seed pod of a pepper, the flowers of broccoli and cauliflower, the root of the carrot.

## Ideas for activities

- Many of the activities listed under vegetable soup (on page 7) support learning for this simple recipe.

## TEACHING POINTS

**Communication, Language and Literacy**

Use talk to organise, sequence and clarify thinking, ideas, feelings and events

Extend their vocabulary

**Knowledge and Understanding of the World**

Look closely at similarities and differences, patterns and change

Ask questions about why things happen and how things work

## What have children learned?

Are children able to notice differences in colour, texture, smell and shape?

Can they see a change as the dip is mixed?

Can they count how many sticks they have cut with one-to-one correspondence? If so, how far?

## Involving parents

Tell parents that you have been examining and exploring vegetables. Encourage them to spend some time in the vegetable section of the supermarket when they next go shopping so that their children can reinforce their learning.

# Bread

Have you ever discovered the joys of making bread by hand? It's a long process but full of satisfaction - the mixing and kneading of the dough, the warm homely aroma that fills the kitchen when the bread is baked, not to mention the delicious taste.

Bread is a universal food, common to most cultures and a staple part of many diets. At its simplest it is flour and water baked, but over centuries it has been developed and fashioned into hundreds of different sorts, shapes, sizes and flavours.

Once you've mastered the basic recipe, you can add extra ingredients or use it as the basis for different types of bread, such as rolls, focaccia or pizza. In this section you'll find recipes from Italy and the Middle East as well as a basic loaf. A trip to a well stocked supermarket will reveal a wide variety of breads which can be used to broaden children's tastes and experiences.

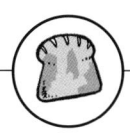

# What you need

### Flour
There are many different types of flour to choose from – white and fine, brown and rough, rye and strong smelling, granary with chunky bits in.

### Yeast
Compressed yeast (usually known as fresh yeast) and dried yeast are different strains of the same species and have different traits. Compressed yeast is a living organism that needs moisture, warmth and flour to stimulate growth. It needs to be stored in the fridge at 4°C or frozen. Compressed yeast is sold in solid form but it can be difficult to find a supplier. If you live near a bakery they may be willing to sell you some. Some health food stores sell it if they have a cold store cabinet.

Instant or fast action dried yeast which comes in sachets is probably easiest to use, although if you are able to obtain fresh, it does make better bread. Dried yeast is available in supermarkets and local stores. It has a much longer shelf life than compressed yeast. The instant sachets need to be mixed into the flour, not the water, whereas fresh yeast should be mixed into some of the tepid water required in each recipe before mixing with the rest of the liquid and added to the flour.

### Salt
Salt adds flavour.

### Water
Water is essential for bread making. It binds the dry ingredients together and enables the yeast to 'work'.

Other ingredients that can be added to the basic bread mixture include:

- Fats, for example butter, olive oil, walnut oil;
- Nuts and seeds, for example walnuts, pumpkin, sesame, poppy and sunflower seeds;
- Fruits, such as dried sultanas, raisins, currants, dates, apricots and prunes for sweet tea breads;
- Cheese, eggs;
- Olives, sun-dried tomatoes, herbs.

### Different types of bread

**Basic daily bread** - white or wholemeal (page 34)

**Flat breads** – unleavened, that is made without yeast, or leavened, such as pitta bread (page 39)

**Italian style breads** – ask children if they know any, such as ciabatta, focaccia (page 38) and pizza (page 41)

**Little breads** – rolls, buns and other different shapes

### Things to do with left-over bread

**Crostini** or toast with toppings

**Panzanella** – bread salad with tomatoes, olive oil, peppers and basil (page 19)

**Bread pudding**

**Breadcrumbs** – apple charlotte (page 68)

# Basic bread

Bread is simple to make from readily available, cheap, raw ingredients. Children may not be able to do all the tasks, but they can shape and knead the dough and they will be fascinated by the changes they see.

Bread making has three main stages which can take up to three hours. However, you could spread the activity over several days.

**Day 1**   Read the recipe with children and make a shopping list. They could make their own using pictures or symbols if they can't yet write.

**Day 2**   Go to the shops or store cupboard to collect the ingredients and look at them in detail. The sugar and flour are the same colour but do they feel and taste the same?

**Day 3**   Make the dough. If there is not enough time for cooking, you could cook the bread later and have it ready for snack time next day.

## Method

Mix the flour (saving a little for dusting) with the salt in a bowl, and if using instant yeast add this too. If using fresh yeast, mix it with half the water in a small bowl until it becomes liquid.

Add this liquid (or water if using instant yeast) to the flour and begin stirring with a wooden spoon or hands, adding more water until a rough dough is formed. Knead together with hands in a bowl, then turn out onto a table and knead for 5-10 minutes until smooth. Show children how to knead and let each one have a go.

Place the dough in a cleaned and oiled bowl, cover with cling-film and leave in a warm place for an hour or so until doubled in bulk.

Turn out and knead again to remove any air (which would cause holes in the bread). If making tin loaves, divide into 3 pieces. Knead each piece and form into an oblong, fold over into a sausage shape and put into greased tins with the fold at the bottom. Dust lightly with flour and cover with cling-film.

For country style bread, divide the dough into 4. Knead each piece into a round and then roll and flatten slightly. Dust baking trays with flour, put rounds on and cover with cling-film.

Leave to rise until about half as big again. During this time heat oven to 400°F/200°C/Gas 6.

Slash the top of country loaves when ready to bake with sharp knife in criss-cross pattern.

Turn oven up to 450°F/230°C/Gas 8 and bake bread for 20–30 minutes until golden and hollow sounding when tapped on bottom. Cool on a wire rack.

---

**Ingredients**
lkg strong white flour
30g salt
25g fresh yeast or 14g instant dried yeast
600ml warm water
oil for greasing bowls and tins

**Equipment**
large bowl
small bowl, if using fresh yeast
3 x 500g loaf tins or flat trays
wooden spoons
measuring jug
rolling pins (optional)
cling-film
table for kneading
knife for cutting dough

**Oven:** 400°F/200°C/Gas 6

**Preparation time:**

Weighing and mixing ingredients 15 minutes

Resting time for dough 60–90 minutes

Second kneading, shaping and proving 30 minutes

**Cooking time:**   30 minutes

## Learning points

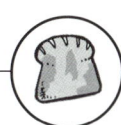

**Words you can use:** knead, dissolve, frothy, elastic, stretchy

Ask children to watch the change as the yeast begins to dissolve into the water. You could talk about other substances that dissolve, for example sugar in tea.

Watch as the yeast begins to froth and bubble. Tell them that yeast is the ingredient that makes the bread light and airy. You could compare this with chapattis which are unleavened and contain no yeast.

Talk about what the dough feels like as they knead it. They should notice a change as it becomes more elastic. If it is too sticky, add more flour (on hands and on tabletop). How is the dough different from playdough? Can they smell the dough?

Explain that the dough needs to be kept in a warm place for the yeast to work and for it to double in size. Ask children to see where

## TEACHING POINTS

**Communication, Language and Literacy**

Use talk to organise and clarify thinking, ideas, feelings and events

Extend their vocabulary

**Mathematical Development**

Use words such as 'more', 'less', 'heavier' and 'lighter'

**Knowledge and Understanding of the World**

Investigate objects and materials using all their senses (as appropriate)

Look closely at similarities and differences, patterns and change

Ask questions about why things happen and how things work

**Physical Development**

Handle malleable materials with increasing control

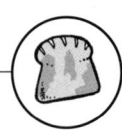

the dough comes to on the side of the bowl. You could measure the side of the bowl with a horizontal hand, for example four fingers from the top, and then measure it again later when the dough has risen.

When the bread is cool enough to eat, talk about slicing and sharing it. If you are making sandwiches you can bring maths into the conversation. How many slices do you need to make a sandwich? How many sandwiches will each person want? How do we cut the sandwiches into halves and quarters or into squares and triangles?

If you decide to make toast, help children to see how the bread changes. Is it the same colour/temperature/texture and does it sound the same when you eat it? What is it that has made the change happen? What happens if you put butter on cold toast as compared with hot toast?

### Culture and beliefs
At the festival of Passover or Pesach Jews celebrate their ancestors' escape from Egypt. Led by Moses, the Jews escaped so quickly that they didn't have time to make proper bread with yeast, so instead they made flat or unleavened bread. During the eight days of Pesach, Jews eat flat bread.

## Ideas for activities

- Read the traditional tale of 'The Little Red Hen' (Ladybird) or the Picture Puffin version by Margot Zemach. The little red hen wants her friends to help her make bread but they only want to help her with the eating. This story can help you talk about sharing the work as well as sharing the prize!

- Make a simple book or wall picture with children's drawings/paintings of the sequence of events in the story of 'The Little Red Hen'.

- Is there a watermill or windmill nearby which you could find out about or visit?

- Sing 'This is the way we make our bread' to the tune of 'Here we go round the mulberry bush'. Verses could include 'This is the way we mix the yeast/knead the dough/make the loaves' all with appropriate actions to match.

- Go to your local supermarket or baker's to see a range of breads or make a collection of different breads which children can look at and sample. Try to find breads from other cultures, such as pitta bread from the Middle East, Asian naan or chapattis, ciabatta from Italy, baguettes from France.

### TEACHING POINTS

**What have children learned?**

Do children notice changes that take place? (dissolving and frothing yeast, expanding and stretchy dough)

Are they beginning to use the new words you have introduced?

Do they manipulate the dough with increasing control?

Are they able to take turns and are they interested to try new activities?

Are older children able to identify or use the numbers on the weighing scales or use any other mathematical language?

Are they showing an interest in the words in the recipe?

Are they able to retell and sequence the main points of action?

Are they able to predict what might happen as you begin to mix ingredients together?

- In summer you could collect small samples of corn - wheat, barley or oats. Look at the different shapes of the corn. Separate the seeds from the stalks and grind them in a pestle and mortar or use a wooden mallet to squash the seeds to make a rough flour. This could be added to any flour you use in your cookery sessions.

- Play baker's shops. Use a salt dough recipe for making the bread and cakes (see below). For the baking section you will need lots of utensils, spoons, bowls and baking tins, baker's hats and aprons, an oven or an old cardboard box on its side. For the shop section you will need money and a till, salt dough breads and cakes and old paper bags.

### TEACHING POINTS

Ask children to bring a slice of bread from home, preferably in a named, small, clear plastic bag. The chances are that there will be many similarities and differences: the colour of the crust, the size and shape, pre-sliced and home sliced, multigrain. After looking at all the differences, the bread could be used to feed birds (in winter only as bread is not good for young birds), eaten at snack time as part of a sandwich or as toast, or left to grow mould for further investigation!

# How to make salt dough

**Ingredients**
2 cups of plain flour
1 cup of table salt
1 cup of water

**Optional:**
1 tablespoon of vegetable oil (makes it a little easier to knead)
1 tablespoon of wallpaper paste (gives the mixture more elasticity)

There are many variations on this simple recipe – you may need to experiment until you get exactly what you want.

## Method

Put the flour, salt and any of the optional ingredients into a mixing bowl and gradually add the water, mixing to a soft dough. If it's too sticky, add more flour, too dry or crumbly, add more water. Place on a flat surface and knead for 10 minutes until smooth. Unused dough can be stored in the fridge, in an airtight container or cling-film, for a couple of days. Children love making models, and as long as you don't add wallpaper paste all of the ingredients are natural, so if they are tempted to put it in their mouths, all it will do is taste salty.

If you want coloured dough, mix food colouring or paint into the water before adding it to the dry ingredients. Or you can paint your creations after baking them at 200°C (no hotter as it can cause cracks or bubbles in the dough). Baking times will vary depending on the size and thickness of the object, but make sure that all of it is hard. If the dough starts to darken before cooking is complete, cover with aluminium foil. You can leave dough to dry naturally but it can take a couple of days.

If you want to keep your crafts, you need to seal them on all sides with clear varnish or polyurethane spray.

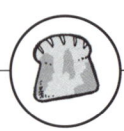

# Focaccia

This Italian bread is enriched with olive oil and can be flavoured with herbs, olives or sun-dried tomatoes. It is good as a snack with raw vegetables or salads.

## Method
Follow the basic bread recipe (on page 34), adding oil and rosemary with the water. Leave to rise at warm room temperature for 40 minutes or until doubled in size.

Punch down and knead dough briefly then push into tin(s). Cover with oiled cling-film and leave to double again.

Make indentations with fingers on top of bread and brush with the water/oil mix. Bake for 20 to 30 minutes until golden and crisp.

## Learning points
See basic bread recipe (pages 34-37) for learning points and activities.

---

**Ingredients**
500g strong bread flour
15g fresh yeast or 7g sachet instant dried yeast
250ml tepid water
60ml olive oil
1tsp salt
2 sprigs fresh rosemary, leaves pulled from stalk and finely chopped
1tbsp olive oil and 1tbsp water mixed together for top of loaf

**Equipment**
mixing bowl
wooden spoons
teaspoon
roasting tin measuring 30 x 40cm or 2 x 20cm sponge cake tins

**Oven:** 425°F/220°C/Gas 7

**Preparation time:**
Mixing ingredients and kneading 15 minutes

First proving 40 minutes

Second kneading, shaping and proving 30 minutes

**Cooking time:**
20–30 minutes

# Pitta bread

**Ingredients**
500g strong flour plus a little extra for dusting
15g fresh yeast or 7g dried
300ml tepid water
1 tsp salt
1/2 tsp sugar
1 tbsp olive oil

**Equipment**
mixing bowl
knife
wooden spoon
cling-film
flat baking sheet
measuring jug
rolling pins
tea cloth
teaspoon
tablespoon

**Oven:** 425°F/220°C/Gas 7

**Preparation time:**

20 minutes plus 60 to 80 minutes for rising

10 minutes rolling

**Cooking time:** 8-10 minutes

These flat breads are handy for dips or as pockets for salads. The children should enjoy rolling them flat and seeing them puff up in the oven.

## Method

If using fresh yeast, mix it with a little of the water and sugar and leave for a few minutes to froth.

Place the flour and salt (and dried yeast if using) in the bowl. Stir in the water, oil and yeast mixture. Stir to mix until it comes together, then turn out onto a clean surface and knead, as in basic bread recipe, for 10 minutes.

Oil the bowl and turn the dough into it. Cover with cling-film and leave in a warm place for an hour or so until risen.

Punch down and cut into 12 pieces. Show children how to roll the dough into a flat oval or circle, using a little flour on the surface and the rolling pin.

Place the pittas on an oiled tray and dust with flour. This will have to be done in batches.

Bake for about 8 minutes and wrap in a cloth to keep them soft. Use straightaway or freeze and re-heat.

COOK AND LEARN TOGETHER

## Learning points

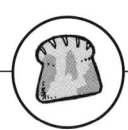

**Words you can use:** dissolve, frothy, dough, knead, elastic, stretchy, pocket

As for basic bread recipe (page 34), but also:

Children will enjoy punching the air out of the dough. Talk to them about the shapes they are making as they roll ovals or circles.

Tell children that the oil on the tray prevents the bread from sticking.

As you set the timer, help children to gain a sense of time passing by talking about the sorts of things you could do in 8 minutes.

## Ideas for activities

- Some children like putting things inside pockets and containers. Extend the theme of pockets by asking children to show what they have in their pockets.

- Make some pocket size feely bags. Place objects inside for children to feel and explore. Ask them to guess what the objects are just by feeling.

## TEACHING POINTS

### What have children learned?

Do children notice changes that take place? (dissolving and frothing yeast, expanding and stretchy dough)

Are they beginning to use the new words you have introduced?

Do they manipulate the dough with increasing control?

Are they able to take turns and are they interested to try new activities?

Are older children able to identify or use the numbers on the weighing scales or use any other mathematical language?

Are they able to link this activity to other experiences they might have had, for example cooking at home, making playdough, visiting a baker's?

Are they showing an interest in the words in the recipe?

Are they able to retell and sequence the main points of action?

Are they able to predict what might happen as you begin to mix ingredients together?

# Pizza

**Ingredients for base**
500g strong flour
15g fresh yeast or 7g instant dried yeast
250ml tepid water
25ml olive oil
1tsp salt

**Ingredients for topping**
tomato sauce, home-made or bought
mozzarella cheese or other suitable melting cheeses

Selection of any of the following:
thinly sliced mushrooms
olives
sliced red peppers
ham or salami

**Equipment**
mixing bowl
wooden spoons
measuring jug
flat baking tray, the largest that will fit in the oven

**Oven:** 450°F/230°C/Gas 8

**Preparation time:**
10 minutes mixing, 30 minutes rising, 15 minutes rolling and assembly

**Cooking time:** 10-15 minutes

Most children love pizza, especially when they have chosen their own topping. It can be eaten hot or cold and it is good to take on a picnic. Pizza originated as a cheap form of food in Italy. It is now widely available with a range of toppings.

## Method

Follow the basic bread recipe (see page 34) adding the olive oil with the water and leave to rise.

Talk about the topping ingredients and let children prepare the things they would like on their pizzas. Give each child a plate to keep their toppings on and cover with cling-film while you wait for the dough to rise.

When the dough is ready to roll out, cut it into pieces about the size of an orange and let each child knead their own dough for a minute before rolling it out using a rolling pin, into a 15cm circle. Place the circles on a greased baking tray.

Give each child some tomato sauce to spread on the base, and then let them choose and arrange their vegetables/meat on top. Slice or grate the cheese and cover the top of the pizza.

Leave to rest for 5 minutes and then cook in the oven, heated as hot as possible, for 10 minutes or until bubbling and smelling delicious.

Let the pizza cool for a minute or so. Cut and serve or cool completely and wrap in foil to eat later.

## Learning points

This recipe has much in common with the basic bread recipe on page 34 so the learning points and activities will be similar. Decorating the pizza offers children plenty of opportunities to be creative, exploring colour, texture and shape.

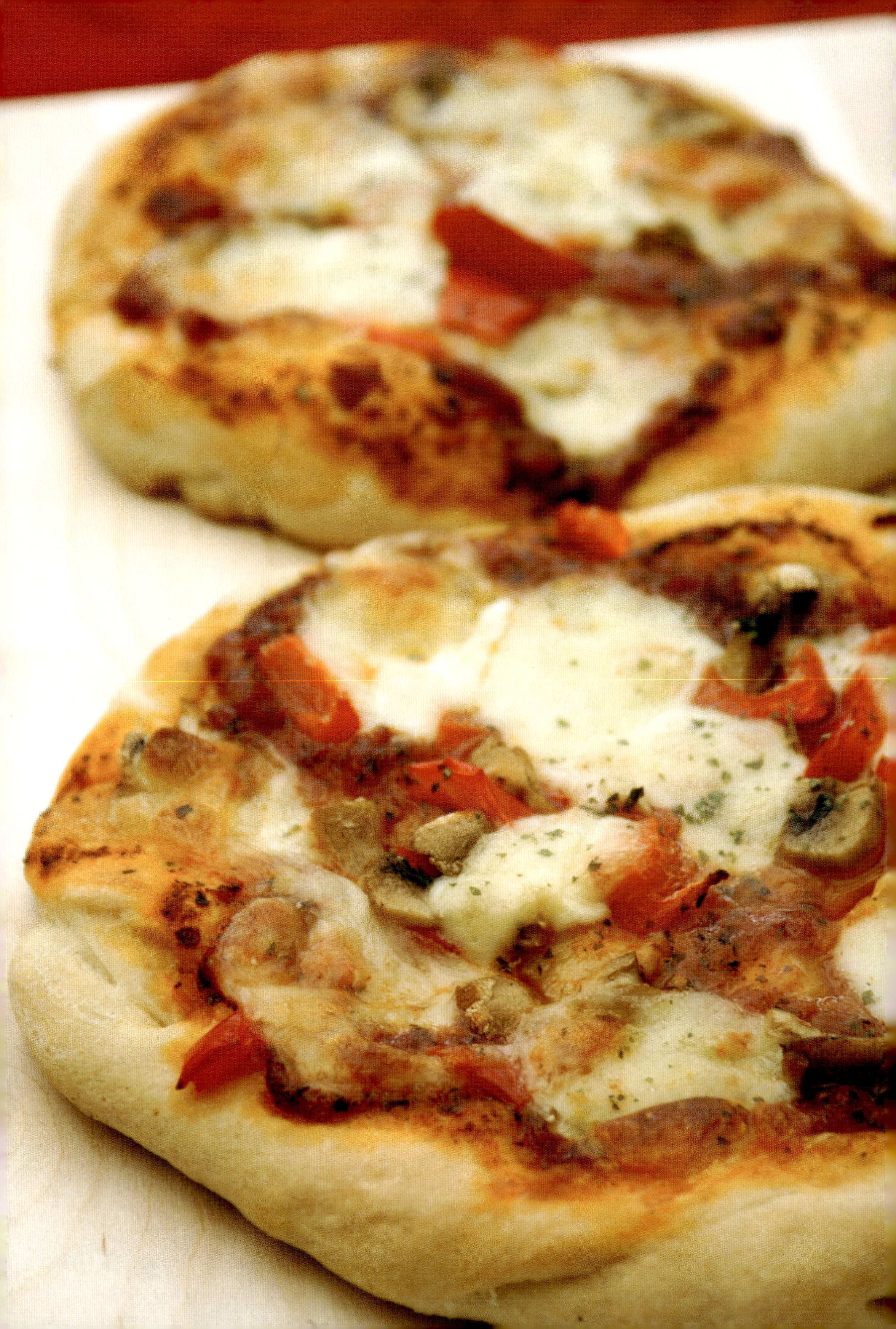

# Hot cross buns

### Ingredients
**(Makes 18 buns)**
750g strong bread flour
120g soft brown sugar
1tsp salt
375ml tepid milk
1tbsp mixed ground spice
2 small eggs
110g butter, melted
200g mixed dried fruit
25g fresh yeast (14g instant dried)
1tsp ground cinnamon
extra flour for kneading
sugar syrup to finish: 3tbsp sugar dissolved in 3tbsp boiling water

### Equipment
large mixing bowl
kettle or other means of boiling water
wooden spoon
teaspoon
tablespoon
baking tray
cooling rack
knife to mark crosses

**Oven:** preheat to 425°F/220°C/Gas 7

**Preparation time:**

25 minutes plus 1 hour rising time

10 minutes shaping plus 30 minutes proving

**Cooking time:** 20 minutes

**Total time:** 2 to 3 hours

Although traditionally eaten on Good Friday, fresh from the oven, these buns can be made in the week leading up to Easter - or any time you like!

### Method

Mix the flour, salt, spices and sugar in a bowl. Add the dried yeast to the flour or dissolve the fresh yeast in a little of the milk. Make a well in the centre of the flour and pour in the milk, plus yeasty milk, beaten eggs and butter. Stir with a wooden spoon until most of the flour is incorporated.

Now gather the dough together with your hands and tip out onto a lightly floured surface. Show children how to knead by pulling and pushing with the ball of the hand. Let each child have a turn, adding a little more flour to the surface if the dough becomes too sticky. Keep going for a total of 12 minutes, by which time the dough should be smooth and elastic.

Put the dough back into the cleaned bowl, cover with cling-film and leave to rise in a warm place for about an hour.

Knock the risen dough out onto a floured surface and punch it out to a flattened shape.

> ### Nursery rhyme
>
> Hot cross buns, hot cross buns,
>
> One a penny, two a penny, hot cross buns.
>
> If you have no daughters, give them to your sons,
>
> One a penny, two a penny, hot cross buns.

**Words you can use:** spices, dissolve, dough, knead, sticky, stretchy, elastic, smooth, flatten

Mix in the fruit and knead well. Divide into 18 pieces and let children shape them into rounds. Place on a well greased baking tray, allowing room between each one for expansion. Cover and leave to rise until doubled in size again, about 30 minutes.

Mark a cross on each bun and bake for 15 to 20 minutes. Explain to children that they are called hot cross buns because they have the mark of a cross on them.

Glaze with sugar syrup. Transfer to cooling rack.

### Learning points

This recipe has much in common with the basic bread recipe (see pages 34-37) and so the learning points and related activities will be similar.

When making this recipe you can sing 'Hot cross buns'.

# Pastry

In this chapter you'll find recipes for sweet and savoury pastry. Most of them recommend a chilled or frozen pastry but if you have time and you need shortcrust pastry, there is nothing quite like the sensory experience of rubbing fat into flour and working the crumbs into a ball of pastry.

Pastry chefs try not to handle pastry too heavily and they work in a cool place to help pastry stay light and flaky. Young pastry cooks may find this difficult but explain that very hot 'heavy' hands will produce a sticky and rather grey pastry!

Pastry making helps to develop the strong finger muscles needed for successful handwriting.

A basic shortcrust pastry recipe suitable for making jam tarts would include 100g plain flour to 50g fat which could be all margarine or butter or half butter, half lard, a pinch of salt and a little cold water. Follow the method as given in little savoury tarts on page 46.

# Little savoury tarts

**Ingredients**
80g mature Cheddar cheese
80g butter
210g plain flour plus a little extra for dusting
iced water
a small onion
half a red pepper
60g mushrooms
4 skinned tomatoes
2 courgettes
1 tbsp vegetable oil
2 tbsp grated fresh Parmesan

**Equipment**
12 or 6 hole bun tins (to suit size of oven)
rolling pins
mixing bowl
pastry cutters (round) to fit bun size
grater
frying pan
knives and forks, slotted spoon
chopping board

**Oven:** 200°C/400°F/Gas 6

**Preparation time:**
25 minutes

As the pastry has to rest, it's best to make it the night before or, if you want children to make it, two sessions will be needed with time for the pastry to rest for one hour in the refrigerator and half an hour for it to return to room temperature before the children roll it.

**Cooking time**: 15 minutes

These tarts are the savoury version of jam tarts. They take longer to make but are a healthier snack. The filling ingredients can be changed for convenience or to suit individual tastes. They are a good addition for a picnic and would go well with a tomato and cucumber salad.

## Method

To make the pastry, rub the butter into the flour until it looks like breadcrumbs.

Grate the cheese and mix it in with a fork. Add iced water a teaspoon at a time until the pastry is formed. Leave to rest in the fridge.

Help children to prepare the vegetables. Each child can prepare a different item. The onion should be chopped as finely as possible. Skin the tomatoes by soaking them for about 1 minute in a bowl of boiling water. Slice when cool. Chop the mushrooms, courgettes and pepper.

Heat the oil in a pan and cook the onions over a low heat until soft. Remove with a slotted spoon on to a large plate. Cook the mushrooms, courgettes and pepper until they are softened a little. Remove to the same plate and allow to cool.

Help children to roll out the pastry and cut rounds with the cutter, placing them in bun trays.

Share the vegetables out evenly between the pastry tarts, placing the sliced tomatoes on top.

Now sprinkle the Parmesan on each tart.

Bake for 12 to 16 minutes until the pastry is cooked and the filling is golden. Allow to cool.

## Learning points

**Words you can use:** vegetables (mushroom, courgette, pepper), pastry, roll, slice, rub, soft, bigger, thinner, flatter

As the children rub the butter into the flour with their fingertips, talk about the textures they can feel - the slipperiness of the butter, the softness of the flour. The flour sticks to the butter to make the 'breadcrumbs'. Eventually, as you add the water, all the little bits join up to make one lump of pastry.

Help children to grate the cheese, making sure they do not grate their fingers in the process! This time children will be taking one lump, the cheese, and making it into lots of little gratings.

As you chop and slice the vegetables, compare their size, colour and texture. Do some

### TEACHING POINTS

**Communication, Language and Literacy**
Use talk to organise, sequence and clarify thinking, ideas, feelings and events

Extend their vocabulary

**Mathematical Development**
Say and use number names in order

**Knowledge and Understanding of the World**
Look closely at similarities and differences, patterns and change

Ask questions about why things happen and how things work

COOK AND LEARN TOGETHER

counting as you prepare the vegetables.

Draw children's attention to how the vegetables soften when they are cooked.

When rolling the pastry, ask children about what is happening. Listen out for the words 'thinner', 'flatter', 'smoother', 'bigger'.

Encourage children to count as they cut their tarts. How many will there be altogether? What is the pattern of the bun tray - four by three to make twelve or two by three to make six?

As you spoon the cooked vegetables into the pastry cases, ask children if they can tell which are onions or peppers or mushrooms.

## Ideas for activities

- Give children a bun tray and some paper cases so that they can practise matching and counting as they play.

- Sing and act out the well-known nursery rhyme 'The Queen of Hearts'.

## TEACHING POINTS

### What have children learned?

Are children able to describe the textures of butter, flour and vegetables?

Can they use mathematical language to describe what happens to the pastry as it is rolled?

Can they count, matching accurately the number name to the correct number of objects? How far can they count?

Do they notice the pattern in the bun tray, for example rows of four with three in each row? When the tray is turned ninety degrees, do they see three rows of four?

### Involving parents

If the tarts are to be taken home, ask parents to talk to their children about who will eat the tarts and how they might be shared.

### Nursery rhyme

The Queen of Hearts
She made some tarts,
All on a summer's day.
The Knave of Hearts
He stole the tarts,
And took them clean away!

The King of Hearts
Called for the tarts,
And beat the knave full score.
The Knave of Hearts
Brought back the tarts,
And vowed he'd steal no more.

# Eccles cakes

### Ingredients
450g ready-made puff pastry

### Filling
30g butter
160g currants
40g chopped mixed peel
75g soft brown sugar
grated zest of I lemon
1 tsp ground ginger
1 tsp grated nutmeg
1 tsp ground cinnamon
1 tbsp lemon juice

### Glaze
1 egg white, lightly whisked
caster sugar

### Equipment
rolling pins
baking sheets
small saucepan
11-13 cm pastry cutter, saucer or template
pastry brush
cup
dessertspoons

**Oven:** 425°F/220°C/Gas 7

**Preparation time:**
35 minutes

**Cooking time:**
20–25 minutes

Eccles cakes are traditional cakes similar to Banbury or Chorley cakes. In this recipe there will be lots of opportunities for children to practise rolling and cutting pastry as well as develop their understanding of quantity by measuring with spoons. As the spices are mixed and warmed children will begin to notice a delicious smell.

## Method

Dust the surface with flour and roll pastry out to the thickness of a £1 coin, then cut out rounds. You will need about 12 cut circles. The trimmings can be reused. Set circles aside to rest.

Melt the butter in a saucepan, then stir in all the filling ingredients. Place spoonfuls in the centre of the rounds.

Brush edges with water and pull pastry up and pinch over the filling.

Turn these balls over and roll gently with a rolling pin until the fruit starts to show through. Make three small parallel cuts in the middle of each.

Place on a wet baking tray.

Brush with beaten egg white and sprinkle lightly with caster sugar. Bake for about 20 minutes until golden.

## Learning points

> **Words you can use**: circle, spices, names of the different sizes and shapes of spoons (teaspoon, tablespoon, dessertspoon)

Count the number of circles. Talk about the curved sides of the circles and the shapes that are left behind as the circles are lifted out. Do these strange shapes look like other objects or animals? Can you cut out circles without leaving any spare bits of pastry? What about squares? Or triangles?

As you add the currants and peel, explain that currants are dried grapes and that peel comes from the skin of oranges and lemons. Nutmeg, cinnamon and ginger are all parts of plants. Nutmeg is the seed of a tree, cinnamon is the inner bark, and ginger is a root.

As the ingredients are heated, ask children if they can smell a spicy aroma.

There are more opportunities for counting as they match a spoonful of mixture to each pastry circle. How many have they done? How many are left to do?

When making the glaze, look at the egg white before and after whisking. Ask children about the changes.

### Older children

Are older children able to recognise that when cutting out circles there will always be scraps left over? (Circles do not tessellate.) Can they work out which shapes would leave no scraps?

Do they know that it is air being whisked into egg white that makes it bubbly and frothy?

Are they able, with help, to calculate how many cakes they will need for the group?

## Ideas for activities

- Make some playdough (see page 52) and provide a range of different shaped cutters - circles, squares, rectangles. Younger children can practise rolling and cutting out. Older children can experiment, trying to cut out shapes without leaving any scraps by using square and rectangular cutters.

- Find some pictures, fabrics, wrapping paper or patchwork to show how shapes can be used over and over to make a pattern. Use sets of squares, rectangles, triangle and circles to find those that will fit together without leaving any spaces (tessellation).

- Make a collection of foods that have distinctive smells. As well as the ones in the recipe you could find cloves, cumin and cardamom or a collection of

### TEACHING POINTS

**Communication, Language and Literacy**
Use talk to organise, sequence and clarify thinking, ideas, feelings and events

Extend their vocabulary

**Mathematical Development**
Say and use number names, counting to ten.

Use language such as 'more', 'less', 'circle', 'bigger', 'smaller'

**Knowledge and Understanding of the World**
Investigate objects and materials by using all their senses as appropriate

Look closely at similarities and differences, patterns and change

Ask questions about why things happen and how things work

**Physical Development**
Handle tools with increasing control

herbs such as mint, basil, parsley or thyme. The herbs and spices will release their scent more strongly when crushed. Can children begin to identify one or two by smell?

- Place a hand whisk and rotary whisk in a bowl of water with a little bubble bath mixture. Children can repeat the whisking action used to make the egg white glaze. Talk about whisking air into the water.

- Use three different sized spoons - tablespoon, dessertspoon and teaspoon - for spooning a range of ingredients (sand, peat, rice, water) into different sized containers.

## Song

Five Eccles cakes in a baker's shop,
Big and round with sugar on the top.
Along came (name of a child)… with a penny one day,
Bought an Eccles cake and took it right away.

**This may be played with fingers or by having five children to represent the cakes and another child with a penny.**

## Action rhyme

Two little eyes to look around,
Two little ears to hear each sound,
One little nose to smell what's sweet,
One little mouth that likes to eat.

**Point to each feature as it is mentioned with particular emphasis on smelling what is sweet – cooking Eccles cakes!**

## TEACHING POINTS

### What have children learned?

Can children count the number of pastry circles? Do they know they are circles?

Can they distinguish between the different sizes of spoons?

Can they match one spoonful of mixture to each circle of pastry?

### Involving parents

Encourage parents to go for a spoon hunt around the kitchen. There will be many different shapes and sizes to compare - wooden spoons, draining spoons, spaghetti spoons, ladles, measuring spoons for cooking, medicine spoons as well as the usual teaspoons, dessertspoons and tablespoons.

Ask them to talk about the different purposes for the spoons, their shapes and sizes, and the different materials from which they are made. Children could play with them in the bath or, if the weather is fine, outside with a bowl of water.

# Flaky mushroom and cheese tarts

**Ingredients**
300g ready-made puff pastry
200g mushrooms
75g cheddar cheese
25g butter
salt/pepper

**Equipment**
baking sheet
rolling pins
frying pan
chopping board
knives
cheese grater

**Oven:** 425°F/215°C/Gas 7

**Preparation time:**
30 minutes

**Cooking time:**
15–20 minutes

These delicious flaky tarts can be eaten warm or cold. Be sure to have plenty of paper napkins to hand to catch the crumbs! Children will be able to experience how cheese changes its shape when grated and then melted. The pastry needs to be kept chilled, so this recipe only works if you have a refrigerator.

## Method

Wash and slice the mushrooms as thinly as possible. Melt the butter in a frying pan, tip in the mushrooms, cook until their juices run out and they are golden. Season with salt and pepper and leave to cool.

Help children to grate the cheese.

Cut the pastry into six pieces and roll out each piece on a well floured surface. Keep each rolled out piece squarish and quite thin.

Place these squares onto a greased, damp baking sheet. (Put water on the baking sheet and let the water run off - this will make the sheet damp enough. ) Spoon the mushrooms between them and top with cheese.

Bake for about 15-20 minutes. Reduce the heat halfway through the cooking time.

### How to make playdough

| | | |
|---|---|---|
| 2 cups plain flour | 1 tbsp cooking oil | few drops of colouring |
| 1 cup salt | 2 tsp cream of tartar | 2 cups water |

Mix all the ingredients in a saucepan over a low heat, stirring all the time. Mix the food colouring with the water before adding if you want a consistently strong colour. For a marbled effect, add the colouring separately. Remove from the heat when the mixture leaves the side of the pan. Knead. Store in an airtight container. It should last for a month or two if you keep it in a fridge.

You could add extra ingredients such as cornflour, lentils or glitter to create different textures.

## Learning points

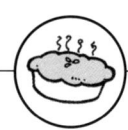

**Words you can use**: slice, roll, square, flat, thin, grater

As children slice the mushrooms, encourage them to look at the shape it makes - if they leave the stalks on they look like little umbrellas. As the mushrooms begin to cook they will release water.

Show children how to hold the grater so that they will not grate their fingers! If you have a box grater there may be four sizes you can choose from so you can talk about the different sized flakes they will make.

To keep the pastry in a square shape the pastry will need to be turned 90 degrees every now and again. This means lifting up the pastry and that is why the surface must be well floured. Tell children that if they press too hard with the rolling pin on an un-floured surface they won't be able to lift the pastry.

Talk about making a little pile of mushrooms and cheese on each square of pastry. Ask children what they think the cheese will look like when it's cooked. Will it still look grated?

## Ideas for activities

- Use a box of shapes to sort squares from oblongs.

- Give children some playdough and any kitchen implements which will help them to change a lump into smaller pieces, for example a grater (supervision will be needed), a garlic press, sieve and colander.

- Do some printing with vegetables and include mushrooms with stalks to create umbrella or tree-like shapes.

## TEACHING POINTS

**Communication, Language and Literacy**
Use talk to organise, sequence and clarify thinking, ideas, feelings and events

Extend their vocabulary

**Mathematical Development**
Use language such as 'bigger' and 'square' to describe the shape and size of flat shapes

**Knowledge and Understanding of the World**
Look closely at similarities and differences, patterns and change

Ask questions about why things happen and how things work

**Physical Development**
Handle tools with increasing control

### What have children learned?

Do children recognise and name a square?

Can they recite and count up to six?

Do they notice the changes in the mushrooms and the cheese?

Do older children recognise that the more they roll the pastry the thinner it becomes?

Do they understand that the flour stops the pastry from sticking to the surface when it is rolled?

# Fish parcels

### Ingredients
300g salmon fillet (organic if possible) or other fish of choice
350g ready-made puff pastry (chilled or frozen which has been allowed to thaw)
a few stalks of parsley and tarragon
salt, pepper and nutmeg
2 tsp lemon juice
egg wash (small egg beaten with a teaspoon of water)

### Equipment
flat baking tray
pastry brush
small bowl or cup
rolling pins
knife and fork

**Oven:** 200°C/400°F/Gas 6

**Preparation time:** 20-25 minutes

**Cooking time:** 20 minutes

Children love to wrap objects up into surprise parcels. These parcels are made of pastry and have fish inside. Ready-made chilled or frozen pastry helps to cut down the preparation time although you could make your own – make it one day, put it in the fridge overnight and use it the following day. Take it out of the fridge to warm up before the children try to roll it out or it will crumble and crack and be difficult to manage.

Many children only eat fish in batter or breadcrumbs. This recipe will tempt them to try something different.

### Method
Divide the fish into 6 pieces. Season each piece with a little grated nutmeg, salt and pepper. Set aside.

Divide the pastry into 6 pieces, sprinkle flour on the table top and show each child how to roll it out into a very thin square.

Place the fish in the middle of the pastry and sprinkle with a little lemon juice.

Brush the edges of the pastry with egg wash and fold over to form a neat parcel, making sure each parcel is sealed by pressing the edges together to keep in the juices.

Place each parcel on an oiled tray and paint with egg wash. Prick the top of each one with a fork to allow the steam to escape.

Bake for about 20 minutes, checking after 15 to make sure they are not browning too much.

Remove from tray and allow to cool.

## Learning points

> **Words you can use:** roll, six, seal, parcels

Tell children that the fish needs to be divided into six. You could start slicing it from one end until you have six pieces or a more challenging way with older children would be to cut it in half and ask them how many more pieces are needed. Each half will need to be cut twice.

Tell children that each piece of fish will need a piece of pastry, so how many pieces of pastry will be needed? This gives you a chance to repeat the experience learned in cutting the fish.

Help children to roll out a square. It might be helpful to have a square cut out of cardboard of the right proportions so they can see what they are trying to make. There are lots of chances with this activity to use words such as 'bigger', 'thinner', 'flatter', 'oblong', 'square'. Remind children not to press too hard otherwise the pastry will stick to the table.

Place the fish in the middle. Most children will understand where the middle is – help those that don't.

The egg wash is used round the edge of the square to act as glue. You can press the parcel together by pushing down with a finger or the end of a spoon or fork. Talk about the pattern it makes.

Egg wash gives the pastry parcel a golden brown colour when it is cooked. Ask children what they think will happen to the fish inside.

Help children to set the timer for 15 minutes which is when the parcels will need checking. When the timer rings, take them to the oven to see if the parcels are ready.

## Ideas for activities

- Sing 'One, two, three, four, five, Once I caught a fish alive'.

- Making parcels – this will be of particular interest to children with enveloping schema (see overleaf).

- Some children enjoy wrapping up old boxes. Provide sticky tape, string, ribbon, glue and a range of materials for wrapping, for example, newspaper, sheet polystyrene, material, tissue paper. Children might like to place objects inside the parcels - give them a few suggestions. Conkers and shells are ideal.

### TEACHING POINTS

**Communication, Language and Literacy**
Use talk to organise, sequence and clarify thinking, ideas, feelings and events

Extend their vocabulary

**Mathematical Development**
Say and use number names in order

Use language such as 'bigger' and 'square' to describe the shapes

**Knowledge and Understanding of the World**
Look closely at similarities and differences, patterns and change

Ask questions about why things happen and how things work

**Physical Development**
Handle tools, objects, construction and malleable materials safely and with increasing control

COOK AND LEARN TOGETHER

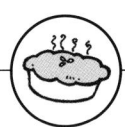

Make underwater collage pictures by drawing fish in wax crayon and using a very thin dilute paint wash (or Brusho) to brush over the fish to create the underwater illusion. This will enable children to repeat the egg wash activity in the recipe.

Visit a nearby fish shop to buy a whole fish – something relatively cheap such as a herring so that children can explore it. Look at the different colours of the scales. Touch them to see how they feel. (If you don't have a fridge you are not likely to want to keep the fish for longer than a day!)

### What are schema?
Schema are patterns of behaviour which become more complex as a child develops. They may be represented in their thinking, language and their play and enable the child to explore the world around them. There are lots of different schema. A child with an enveloping schema, for example, might wrap things around themselves, enjoy dressing up, climb into spaces such as a large cardboard box, do a painting and then wrap it up by folding and refolding or wrap objects in paper.

## TEACHING POINTS

### What have children learned?
Can children use mathematical language – 'bigger', 'smaller', 'square', 'oblong', 'thinner', 'flatter'?

Can they count accurately to six?

Are older children able to solve the problem of dividing the fish and pastry into six by first cutting it in half?

Can children handle the tools and the pastry with appropriate levels of physical control?

### Involving parents
Tell parents that their children have been making fish parcels. Encourage them to let children make parcels at home out of playdough or cheap recycled materials such as boxes and newspaper.

## Nursery rhyme

One, two, three, four, five,
Once I caught a fish alive.
Six, seven, eight, nine, ten,
Then I let it go again.
Why did you let it go?
Because it bit my finger so.
Which finger did it bite?
This little finger on my right!

COOK AND LEARN TOGETHER

# Sausage rolls/ cheesy rolls

Sausage rolls are an old classic. Children will have fun making their own and maybe using the left-over pastry to make some crisp shapes. For those who do not eat meat, the vegetarian version is just as tasty.

## Method

### For sausage rolls

Mix the sausage meat, onion and herbs together in a bowl and then set aside while rolling out the pastry.

Divide the pastry into 4 pieces. Guide children into rolling the pastry into pieces about 30 x 10cm.

On another surface, dusted with flour, roll the sausage meat into 4 lengths the same size as the pastry.

Place these in the centre of each piece of pastry.

Moisten one long edge with water and roll up to enclose the sausage meat, sealing the edge well, and placing the join underneath.

Let each child cut the roll into 4 or 5 pieces with a suitable knife.

Place on a dampened baking tray, brush each one with egg wash and make a couple of small cuts in the top.

Bake for 15 to 20 minutes.

### For cheesy rolls

Grate the cheese, beat the egg and mix with the other ingredients in a bowl.

Proceed in exactly the same way as for the sausage rolls but bake for 12 to 16 minutes.

**Ingredients**
500g ready-made puff or shortcrust pastry
egg wash (1 small egg whisked with 1 tbsp milk)

**Meat filling**
400g good quality sausage meat
1 small onion, finely chopped
1/2 tsp mixed dried herbs

**Vegetarian filling**
250g cheddar cheese
1 small onion, finely chopped
1/2 tsp paprika
1 small egg

**Equipment**
rolling pins
flat baking tray
pastry brush
knives
small basin
mixing bowl

**For cheesy rolls**
grater
mixing bowl
forks

**Oven:** 400°F/200°C/Gas 6

**Preparation time:**
20 minutes

**Cooking time:** 20 minutes

## Learning points

**Words you can use**: roll, larger, smaller, thinner, thicker, longer, shorter, same length as, vegetarian, half, quarter

Talk to children about how they will know when the herbs and onions are mixed in. Ask them to watch carefully as the mixture is stirred.

Dividing the pastry gives an opportunity to talk about fractions. Ask children to divide the mixture into half and then half again to make quarters.

Dusting the surface stops the mixture from sticking. It is the equivalent of dusting hot summer feet with talcum powder so that the soles of your feet don't stick to your shoes! Have another go at cutting ingredients into quarters.

Match one piece of meat to each piece of pastry. If the filling had only been cut in half, how many rolls would have filling and how many would not?

Moistening pastry helps you to join two pieces together. It acts like glue!

Cutting the long roll into 4 or 5 pieces provides plenty of opportunity for mathematical discussion – counting and adding in fours or fives. You could practise halving and halving again. If you want to cut into fives, can you use the same method?

Explain that the egg wash gives the pastry a lovely golden colour. The slits allow some of the steam to escape from the cooking mixture.

Show children how to set the timer. Can they read any of the numbers?

## Ideas for activities

- As with other dishes where pastry is used to wrap another ingredient, this activity is likely to appeal to those children who repeatedly like to put objects inside other objects (known as an enveloping schema – see page 56), for example letters in envelopes, boxes inside boxes, even wrapping themselves up so they cannot be seen, climbing into dens or boxes. Nurture this interest by finding other activities which include an element of envelopment.

- If you have fruit for a snack, repeat the activity of cutting into halves and then into quarters. This is easily done with bananas or apples.

## TEACHING POINTS

**Mathematical Development**
Say number names, counting to ten

Use language such as 'more', 'less', 'circle', 'bigger', 'smaller'

**Knowledge and Understanding of the World**
Investigate objects and materials by using all their senses as appropriate

Look closely at similarities and differences, patterns and change

Ask questions about why things happen and how things work

**Physical Development**
Handle tools with increasing control

## What have children learned?

Can children cut quantities in half then in half again?

Can they use the words 'half' and 'quarter'?

Can they match one piece of filling to each piece of pastry?

Can they use the tools to roll out a piece of pastry to the appropriate size?

## Involving parents

Tell parents that their children have been learning about halves and quarters and ask them to see if there are ways they can help them to further their understanding at home.

# Sausage plait

## Ingredients
250g frozen puff pastry, just thawed
300g good quality sausage meat
3 tomatoes
salt, pepper
1/2 tsp mixed dried herbs
beaten egg to glaze pastry

## Equipment
baking sheet
small mixing bowls
rolling pins
cup for beaten egg
knives
fork

**Oven:** 400°F/200°C/Gas 6

**Preparation time:** 20 minutes

**Cooking time:** 35 minutes

Another old favourite that's great for picnics.

### Method
Place tomatoes in a bowl and cover with boiling water. Leave for a minute; drain, then peel and slice thinly.

Roll out the pastry on a lightly floured surface to an oblong about 28 x 22cm. Spread half the sausage meat in a strip 8cm wide down the centre of pastry.

Arrange the tomato slices on top and season with a little salt, pepper and the herbs. Then place the rest of the sausage meat on top of this.

Cut slits 1 cm apart down the pastry on either side of the filling.

Fold the strips from either side alternately, at an angle across the filling, to give a plaited effect.

Place on a damp baking sheet and brush with the beaten egg. Place in a hot oven to cook for 30 to 35 minutes or until golden and sizzling. Remove and eat or leave to cool for a picnic.

## Learning points

**Words you can use**: plait, filling, pastry, skin, roll, thin, thick

Boiling water enables the skins to be removed easily from the tomatoes. There is little to see in this process but if you try skinning a tomato without the help of boiling water it will take a long time!

Estimate how many slices you will be able to make from one tomato. If you have tomatoes of different sizes ask children if they will get more or fewer slices from the large tomato.

As children roll out the pastry, ask them what is happening. Use words such as 'thick', 'thin' and 'thinner'. Use a ruler to measure the size. Can children recognise the numbers on the ruler?

Sausage meat is, of course, what sausages are made from but without the skin. Help children to judge half the mixture and to shape it into a fat snake along the pastry.

Ask children if they know how to make sure the slits are straight. They may come up with their own ideas – if not you could suggest using the ruler as a firm edge against which to press the knife.

Children will enjoy plaiting the pastry. This will be easy if the pastry is not too sticky or too warm! Talk about other plaits - perhaps some children plait their hair.

Dampening the baking sheet creates a little steam in the hot oven which helps to cook the sausage plait. Talk about steam. They may have noticed the steam from a bath, a kettle or on a hot tarmac road after a summer shower of rain.

## Ideas for activities

- Make some playdough (see page 52) and encourage children to cut into it in a variety of ways to make patterns.

- Give children a variety of materials for plaiting and weaving, for example strips of crepe paper, ribbons and strings of different colours and thickness. If you have a fence, let children use it like a large loom and weave wool or string between the upright bars.

- Have some different types of cord, wool, string and rope for children to examine and explore. Can they see that the rope is made of several strands twisted together? Twisting materials together makes them stronger and can be a way of joining two materials together.

- Do any of your children have their hair braided or plaited in a special way?

## TEACHING POINTS

**Communication, Language and Literacy**
Use talk to organise, sequence and clarify thinking, ideas, feelings and events

**Mathematical Development**
Use language such as 'thinner', 'thicker', 'larger', 'smaller'

Use everyday language to describe position

**Knowledge and Understanding of the World**
Look closely at similarities and differences, patterns and change

Ask questions about why things happen and how things work

**Physical Development**
Handle tools, objects and malleable materials safely and with increasing control

## What have children learned?

Can children use key words in the correct context, for example 'thinner' as they roll out the pastry?

Can they manipulate and plait the pastry?

## Involving parents

Ask parents to help children explore off-cuts of string, wool and rope at home.

Is anyone a hairdresser who could demonstrate braiding and plaiting skills?

# Sausage, tomato and onion pie

**Ingredients**
400-500g ready-made pastry
extra flour for dusting
or
250g plain flour
60g lard
70g butter
cold water to mix

500g sausage meat
300g tinned, chopped, drained tomatoes
1 large onion, peeled and thinly sliced
1 tsp mixed dried herbs
25ml sunflower oil
1 egg, whisked
salt and pepper

**Equipment**
roasting or baking tray 18 x 25cm
or individual foil pie dishes for children to take home
rolling pins
knives, forks, spoons
mixing bowl for pastry
frying pan
pastry brush
tin opener
cup

**Oven:** 200°C/400°F/Gas 6

**Preparation time:** 20-40 minutes depending on whether you use ready-made pastry

**Cooking time:** 40-50 minutes

This is quite an ambitious recipe for small children but will be very much enjoyed. To cut down the preparation time, you could make the pastry at home or buy a pack of chilled shortcrust pastry.

## Method

To make pastry:

Place the flour in a bowl, cut the lard and butter into small pieces and mix well with flour. Then rub into the flour with fingertips until it looks like breadcrumbs.

Add 1tbsp cold water and mix with a knife, then hands, until it comes together. A little more water may be needed but take care not to make too wet.

Cover with cling-film and leave to rest in a cool place for 30 minutes or overnight.

Slice the onion and cook gently in a frying pan with the oil until softened. Young children may need plenty of help with slicing the onions as they can be slippery and smelly!

Meanwhile, lightly grease the tin.

Dust the work surface with flour and, using just half of the pastry, roll it out slightly larger than tin - with a little overhang. Leave to rest.

Break the sausage meat up with a fork and place half of it on the pastry. Cover with the onions, seasoning, herbs and tomatoes, then put the rest of the sausage meat over this, getting children to make it as flat as possible. Tell children that this is the filling for the pie.

Roll the rest of the pastry to cover. Wet the edge of the pastry in the tin with cold water and press the top down, sealing the edges well. Trim off excess pastry and flute edge or press with a fork. Make two slits in the top and brush with whisked egg.

Bake for 20 minutes at 200°C, and then lower heat to 180°C for 20-30 minutes more until golden and cooked through.

## Learning points

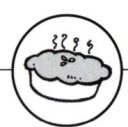

**Words you can use**: roll, fry, whisk

Explain that the tin is greased to stop the pastry from sticking to it when it is cooked.

When rolling out the pastry, ask children when they think the pastry is big enough to fit the tin. They might not realise that they will need enough to cover the bottom, up the sides and still leave a little overhang.

Explain that wetting the edge of the pastry and pressing it together makes a good join. The whisked egg gives the pastry a lovely golden colour when it is cooked. If you leave a few spots of pastry unglazed they will be able to see the difference.

## Ideas for activities

- Roll out a pack of ready-made pastry. Cut into small shapes or strips and invite children to join pieces together using whisked egg and a little pressure. You may have to limit the number of shapes they use to make sure you can fit them all onto a baking sheet. A fish slice would be handy. The shapes can then be cooked on a baking tray for 20 minutes. Children should be able to see the effects of their joining skills!

- Give children cutters, pins and some bun trays and foil pie cases to use with playdough.

## TEACHING POINTS

**Communication, Language and Literacy**
Use talk to organise, sequence and clarify thinking, ideas, feelings and events

Extend their vocabulary

**Knowledge and Understanding of the World**
Look closely at similarities and differences, patterns and change

Ask questions about why things happen and how things work

**Physical Development**
Handle tools with increasing control

## What have children learned?

This recipe involves physical dexterity: rolling, breaking up with a fork, pressing, brushing with a pastry brush. This would be a good recipe to assess children's physical skills in handling tools.

Older children may begin to grasp the reasons why the pastry has to be rolled larger than the bottom of the tin.

## Involving parents

Ask parents to talk with their children about their favourite pies. Pie boxes could be brought in for a role-play shop.

### Nursery rhyme

Simple Simon met a pieman,
Going to the fair.
Said Simple Simon to the pieman,
'Let me taste your ware'.

Said the pieman to Simple Simon,
'Show me first your penny'.
Said Simple Simon to the pieman,
'Indeed I have not any'.

# Puddings

Fruit is an important ingredient for many puddings and desserts. There is an increasing awareness that we need to eat fresh fruit for a healthy and well balanced diet, so what could be better than fruit salad, the contents of which can vary with the seasons. The ingredients for apple charlotte and pancakes are relatively cheap and easy to come by.

# Jelly with fruit

**Ingredients**
1 tablet of jelly (or more, depending on number of children)
assorted fruits: grapes, kiwi, pear, peach, banana or, when in season, raspberries or strawberries
1/2 pint boiling water

**Equipment**
kettle
measuring jug
fruit bowl or small dishes
knives
spoon
basin
fridge

**Time:** 10–15 minutes preparation and talk
5 minutes making jelly
2 hours for jelly to set

You will need a fridge for this recipe. Introduce variations by using different flavoured jellies and choosing different fruits. You can look at how fruits differ from one another in colour, shape, texture and taste.

**Method**
Ask children to cut the fruit into pieces, peeling where necessary, and place in serving bowls.

Break the jelly into cubes, place in a basin and pour over boiling water. Stir until dissolved.

Pour the dissolved jelly mixture over fruit and leave to set in fridge in bowls.

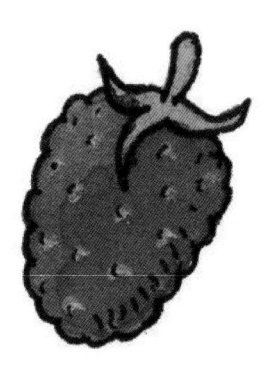

## Learning points

> **Words you can use**: dissolve, skin, seeds, pips, stalk, names of fruit used, transparent, textures of fruit skin (hairy, smooth, bumpy, ridged)

Before children start to cut up the fruit, talk about the shapes, colours and texture of the skins. As they cut up the fruit you will be able to talk about the pips and seeds and the appearance of the flesh. Orange flesh is distinctive and quite different from a banana. You can also talk about which fruits seem to be particularly juicy.

The jelly dissolves into the water. Try to use the right scientific word yourself but don't worry too much if the children use the term 'melt' - just draw their attention to the word you used. Although the jelly tablets seem to disappear they have dissolved into the water. How do we know the jelly tablet is still there? It has turned the water a different colour and it will taste of the fruit flavour of the jelly and not of plain water.

As the jelly mixture is poured over the fruit some of the fruit will float to the top. Does any fruit stay at the bottom? Can they tell the different fruits in the jelly? Help children to understand that you can see through jelly. It is transparent. If the fruit were in custard would they be able to see it so clearly?

## Ideas for activities

- Experiment with some other ingredients to see if they dissolve in hot water. Try white sugar, honey, salt, instant coffee, as well as breakfast cereals and dried fruit. Is it possible to tell just by looking whether it is white sugar or salt that has dissolved in water?

- Find some coloured transparent paper for children to look through - like looking at the world through a jelly!

- Talk about fruit being good for the body. Try to get a book or some leaflets about why we need to eat fresh fruit and vegetables.

## TEACHING POINTS

**Communication, Language and Literacy**
Use talk to organise, sequence and clarify thinking, ideas, feelings and events

Extend their vocabulary

**Knowledge and Understanding of the World**
Look closely at similarities and differences, patterns and change

Ask questions about why things happen and how things work

**Physical Development**
Handle tools with increasing control

### What have children learned?

Can children name some basic parts of the fruit they are cutting? (skin, seeds/pips, flesh, juice)

Do they begin to explain the changes that have happened to the jelly?

Do they notice the springy quality of the jelly as they tear up the tablets?

Older children might be able to talk about the changes in the right sequence: It was hard (a solid), then it dissolved (into a liquid) and when it got cold in the fridge it went hard again (a solid).

COOK AND LEARN TOGETHER

# Fruit salad

### Ingredients
**Autumn fruit salad**
2 crisp apples
4 plums
1 orange
100g blackberries
100g seedless grapes

**Tropical fruit salad**
2 oranges
1 mango
1 small pineapple
2 kiwi fruit
1 small papaya

**Red fruit salad**
100g strawberries
100g raspberries
100g loganberries
100g red cherries
50g redcurrants
Juice of an orange

**Green fruit salad**
100g seedless white grapes
1 green apple
2 kiwi fruit
1 small Galia melon
juice of a lemon
100ml apple juice

### Equipment
chopping board
sharp knife
knives for the children
bowl
lemon squeezer

### Preparation time:
20-30 minutes

You don't really need a recipe for this, but as it is so important for children to eat lots of fruit, this is a good way of getting them to think about different fruits and introduce them to some with which they may not be familiar. Although most fruits can be bought all year round, this is a good chance to talk about seasonality and make the salad with fruit that is in season and locally available.

Here are four different lists of ingredients to choose from, but there are many more variations. One provides an all red salad, another all green. Different shades of the same colour can be discussed together with the different shapes and tastes.

### Method
The fruits for all the variations are prepared in a similar way. Apples, grapes and plums should be washed, but the soft fruits should be fine with just a check over to remove any soft or blemished fruit. Everything else is peeled.

Apples are cut in quarters and the cores removed. Children can then cut them into small pieces.

Oranges: peeled, segmented, each segment cut in half and mixed with the apple to prevent discolouration.

Plums and cherries: cut in half, stones removed, and the plums cut into smaller pieces.

Melon needs to be cut in half, the seeds scooped out with a spoon and discarded. Peel the melon so the children can then cut it into small pieces.

Do the same with the papaya. Kiwi fruit needs peeling and slicing.

Mango is tricky to cut without wasting a lot of the flesh – and messy! Cut lengthwise either side of the stone and then peel and cut the other piece from the stone as best you can.

Pineapple is quite tricky to peel and care must be taken to remove all the 'eyes' from under the skin.

The mango and pineapple (or any similar fruit) can then be cut into pieces by the children.

Soft fruit, apart from strawberries, should be left whole. Strawberries can be cut in half or sliced if they are large.

Add the fruit to the bowl as it is prepared, mixing in the juice where applicable.

Fruit salad should be eaten as soon as possible, although it could be sent home with children if suitable sealed plastic containers are available. The children will be pleased to show at home what they have achieved.

## Learning points

**Words you can use**: skin, seeds, pips, stalk, names of fruit used, transparent, textures of fruit skin (hairy, smooth, bumpy, ridged)

The opportunities for children to talk about shape, size, colour, smell and touch and quantity are endless! Make sure that you allow enough time for children to experience the benefit of using all their senses and to talk and compare one fruit with another.

## Ideas for activities

- Set up a fruit and vegetable shop. Use plastic fruit or make your own using scrunched-up newspaper bound by newspaper bandages and lots of wallpaper paste. Paint the appropriate colour when the glue has dried.

- Using old gardening magazines, make some collage pictures of fruit and vegetables which could be used as posters in a role-play shop.

- In winter, feed blackbirds with the scraps of apple core.

- With older children who are building up their knowledge of letters and the linked sounds, make a fruit alphabet. For example a is for apple, b is for blackberry, c is for currant. If possible, use real fruit and for those out of season use photographs from magazines.

### TEACHING POINTS

Find the most popular fruit in the salad. Find a simple way to record your findings.

### Involving parents

Tell parents that their children have been learning the names of different fruit. Ask them to talk about the fruit they see at the supermarket or fruit and vegetable shop.

# Apple charlotte

## Ingredients
1 small stale white or wholemeal loaf
100g melted butter

**Filling**
1kg apples
50g butter
50g raisins (optional)
zest and juice of a lemon
75-100g sugar
1/2 teaspoon ground cinnamon

**Equipment**
saucepan
bread knife and boards
knives for children
vegetable peeler or paring knife for adults
charlotte mould or 4 individual foil pudding basins
silver foil for wrapping
tablespoon and teaspoon

**Oven:** 200°C/400°F/Gas 6

**Preparation time:** 25 minutes

**Cooking time:** 20 minutes for individual pudding basins, 40 minutes for one large mould

Most of us have left-over bread from time to time and there are many good ways of making use of this. Here is a recipe for a dish which is tasty and comes in many versions. Sometimes the bread is crumbed and layered between the cooked apple but in this one the bread has a crisper finish. In the autumn, you may have windfall apples from the garden that you can use. This could lead to a discussion about how we can use so many things which would otherwise be wasted.

## Method
Cut the crusts off the bread and cut into the thinnest possible slices.

Melt the 100g of butter in a pan. Dip the slices of bread into the butter and line the mould(s), saving enough for the lid(s).

Peel the apples and cut into quarters, removing the cores, and let children cut these into small pieces on their boards.

Melt the 50g of butter in the pan, add the apples and sugar. Cook, stirring occasionally, until soft. Stir in raisins if using, cinnamon, lemon juice and zest.

Spoon into the moulds and cover with the reserved bread. Bake for 20 minutes or longer until golden. Cool and double wrap with foil if sending home.

## Learning points

**Words you can use**: bread, stale, crusts, crumb, dip, mould, half, quarter, core, melt, line

Compare the colour and texture of the crust to the inside of the loaf. The texture of the loaf may vary. In places there may be larger air spaces. If you are making this recipe in winter, keep the crusts to feed to the birds.

As you dip the bread into the butter the slices will become heavier. The butter will quickly be soaked up. Ask children where the butter has gone. Explain what it means to line the mould with bread – this may be the first time they have heard the word 'line' used in this way. Talk about the mould and how their apple charlottes will be the same shape and size as the mould.

Before cutting up the apples compare their colour and size. Can they find where the stalk grew? As the apple is halved and quartered, count the number of pieces you have. Look for and count the seeds around the core.

Help children to identify the changes in the apples as they are cooked.

Count the spoons of apple as they are placed inside the mould. Discuss the size of bread which will be needed to cover the top. Use words that compare size: 'larger', 'smaller', 'wider', 'narrower', 'longer'.

## Ideas for activities

- Use windfall apples to make apple prints with paint. Experiment with cutting the apple horizontally across the centre to see another pattern.

- At Hallowe'en, play a game of apple bobbing by hanging the apples up with string or floating them on water. (This activity is quite difficult and children will need an adult to help them.)

- Put a variety of containers, for example yoghurt pots, in your sand pit or sand tray so that children can understand more about using moulds.

- Make a display of different shapes, sizes and colours of apples. If you know them, use their variety name, for example Cox's orange pippin.

## TEACHING POINTS

**Communication, Language and Literacy**
Use talk to organise, sequence and clarify thinking, ideas, feelings and events

**Mathematical Development**
Say and use number names

Use mathematical ideas and methods to solve practical problems

Use language such as 'smaller' and 'larger' to compare size

**Knowledge and Understanding of the World**
Look closely at similarities and differences, patterns and change

Ask questions about why things happen and how things work

### What have children learned?

Do children notice that the bread absorbs the melted butter?

Can they spot similarities and differences in size and colour between the apples?

Do they use mathematical language to compare the size and shape of the slices?

### Involving parents

Ask parents to spend time peeling, cutting and eating apples at home, or send in an apple for snack time.

# Pancakes

### Ingredients
125g plain flour
pinch of salt
2 eggs, beaten
260ml milk
1 tbsp sunflower oil for frying

1 lemon
1 tbsp caster sugar

### Equipment
sieve
measuring jug
plates
mixing bowl
wooden spoon
small bowl
frying pan 15-17 cm diameter
fish slice or spatula
kitchen paper

### Preparation time:
15 minutes plus cooking

Pancakes are traditionally eaten on Shrove Tuesday which marks the beginning of Lent in the Christian faith. At one time people fasted throughout Lent so they tried to eat up all the rich food in the house. Pancakes were a good way of using up butter and eggs. There are different variations around the world, for example French crepes, Russian blini, American buttermilk pancakes and Mexican tortillas and enchiladas.

Pancakes are often served simply with lemon and sugar but there are lots of fillings, both savoury and sweet, to be explored. Children can be involved with measuring and mixing but will probably only watch the cooking as the frying pan must be very hot to ensure crisp pancakes. The ingredients will make approximately 12 pancakes.

## Method
Sieve the flour and salt into a mixing bowl and make a well in the centre.

Break the eggs into a small bowl and pour them into the well of flour.

Pour in a third of the milk and start mixing, gradually incorporating the flour. Add the rest of the milk in small amounts, beating well after each addition. The finished mixture should be smooth and the consistency of single cream.

Heat the frying pan and wipe over with kitchen paper dipped in oil, completely coating the surface.

Pour some batter into the pan, tilting it to cover the base completely, and cook over fairly high heat until set. Flip over to cook other side briefly. Tip out onto plate and repeat with the rest of the mixture.

Sprinkle with caster sugar and a squeeze of lemon juice, roll or fold and eat while still warm.

## Fillings
**Sweet fillings** - maple syrup, honey, jam, caster sugar or chocolate sauce.

**Fruit fillings** – warm pureed apple, crushed raspberries, strawberries or blueberries with a little whipped cream.

**Savoury fillings** – such as tomato and cream cheese or mushroom and sour cream (see below). These should be prepared before you start to cook the pancakes. Each filling recipe is enough to fill about a dozen pancakes.

### Tomato and cream cheese
700g (approximately 8 medium sized) firm tomatoes
250g of cream cheese
2 tbsp chopped parsley
a little ground pepper

Scald, skin and remove the seeds of the tomatoes. Chop the flesh. Cream the cheese with a little cream or milk. Add the chopped tomatoes, parsley and pepper. Spread about a slightly heaped tablespoon of mixture onto one half of the pancake and roll or fold into half and then quarters. There are good opportunities here to explore shape!

**Mushroom and sour cream**
900g mushrooms
20g butter
1 large onion
3 tbsp chopped parsley
150g sour cream or crème fraiche
juice of a lemon

Finely chop the onion and cook until soft. Wash and finely chop the mushrooms and add to the onions, stirring for about 4 minutes. Add the juice of a lemon and then leave to cool in a bowl. Stir in enough of the cream to make a thick creamy sauce. Add the parsley and season to taste.

When the pancakes are cooked, spread about a slightly heaped tablespoon of mixture onto one half of the pancake and roll or fold into half and then quarters.

## Action rhyme

| | |
|---|---|
| Mix a pancake | (*Mime putting ingredients in*) |
| Stir a pancake | (*Mime stirring a bowl*) |
| Pop it in the pan | (*Mime pouring batter*) |
| Fry the pancake | (*Mime holding a frying pan over the heat*) |
| Toss the pancake | (*Mime throwing it in the air*) |
| Catch it if you can | (*Mime moving the pan around and eventually catching the pancake*) |

## TEACHING POINTS

**Communication Language and Literacy**
Use talk to organise, sequence and clarify thinking, ideas, feelings and events

Extend their vocabulary

**Mathematical Development**
Say and use number names in order

**Knowledge and Understanding of the world**
Look closely at similarities and differences, patterns and change

Ask questions about why things happen and how things work

## Learning points

**Words you can use**: sieve, yolk, well, pancake, roll, fold

As you sift the dry ingredients, ask children to think about why we use a sieve. Are there any lumps left in the sieve? If so, why didn't they go through? What will make the lumps disappear?

Talk about the different parts of the egg, the yolk and the white.

The next step is common procedure for mixing cement! Making a well, allow the dry ingredients to be gradually drawn into the mixture. Draw children's attention to how the mixture changes as more milk is added.

Point out that greasing the pan prevents the mixture from sticking to it.

As you ladle the mixture into the pan, tip the pan slightly so children can see how the mixture moves across the pan until it changes from liquid to solid.

## Ideas for activities

- Read the story of 'The Runaway Chapatti' or 'The Enormous Pancake'.

- Act out the story with small world toys in the sand tray.

- Make the role-play area into a crepe or pancake stall.

- Make card pancakes using brown wax crayon for the browned spots and a dilute yellow paint as a colour wash. These could be used for role play.

## TEACHING POINTS

### What have children learned?

Do children notice the changes as the egg and milk mixture is absorbed by the flour and the mixture is poured into the pan and cooked?

Can they count the number of pancakes that have been made and work out how many each person will have?

Can they talk about the sequence of this simple recipe?

Can they talk about the shapes they see as they roll and fold the pancakes?

### Involving parents

Have a pancake race at your next outdoor fundraising event.

COOK AND LEARN TOGETHER

# Cakes and biscuits

Although the emphasis in our diet should be on fresh meat, fish, vegetables, grains and fruit, cakes and other bakes have their place, especially when homemade. Children will probably be most enthusiastic about this chapter!

Find out who likes cakes and what sort. Who helps to make them? Do they know what it is in the ingredients that make them rise? Talk about the different textures: soft, greasy butter, grainy sugar, dry flour, hard nuts, rough oats, whole firm eggs protected in their shell and then slimy and slippery inside.

Talk about how the ingredients change when they are being mixed and how they change again after baking. This is also a good time to discuss different traditions in a variety of cultures and different festivals and celebrations.

# Chocolate biscuit cake

**Ingredients**
2 tbsp golden syrup
175g butter
125g plain chocolate, broken into pieces
1 tbsp cocoa powder
280g rich tea or digestive biscuits
50g walnuts, chopped
100g sultanas

**Equipment**
shallow cake tin (18cm square or 15 x 20 cm), buttered
bowl
saucepan
tablespoons
strong paper or plastic bag
rolling pin

**Preparation time:**
15 minutes

**Setting time:** 2 –10 hours

**This is a simple recipe that makes an excellent cake for a children's party. The walnuts can easily be left out if there are children with allergies to nuts and could be replaced by cherries.**

## Method

Melt the syrup, butter, chocolate and cocoa in a bowl over a saucepan of hot water and stir.

Put the biscuits in a paper bag, a few at a time and let children crush them with the rolling pin. Repeat until all the biscuits are crumbs.

Add nuts, sultanas and crumbs to the chocolate mix and spread in a buttered tin, smoothing and pressing the top.

Put in a cool place to set (preferably a refrigerator) and cut into small squares.

## Learning points

**Words you can use:** melt, hot, stir, warm, cool, set, crush, crumbs, spread

Tell children that you will need to melt some ingredients together. If possible, let them watch the whole process. Ask them which ingredient seem to change the fastest. Explain that you are using a bowl because you do not want the mixture to get too hot. Compare the melted chocolate in the bowl and any pieces of solid chocolate you have left over. Do they think the taste of the chocolate will have changed?

Encourage children to listen to the sound of the biscuits breaking as they roll the pin over the bag. If you use a clear plastic bag they will be able to see the crumbs getting smaller and smaller. Help them to notice this.

Ask children to watch as you mix the ingredients together. Let them stir the mixture. They should feel it getting thicker and more difficult to stir. Explain that buttering the tin helps to prevent the cake from sticking to it.

Explain that the cake must go hard before they can eat it. Involve children in finding the coldest place to leave it to set. How will they be able to tell that the cake is ready? How could they test that the cake has set?

When the cake is ready to eat, ask them what they think will happen to the chocolate as the cake goes into their warm mouths. The children will be learning that some changes are temporary and reversible (see page 106).

## Ideas for activities

- Explore other substances that will melt by placing them in the sun or a warm place, for example on a radiator. You could try butter, chocolate, an ice cube or ice cream. All these ingredients will change from solids to liquids, some faster than others. Once melted they can be placed in the fridge or freezer compartment so that further change can be observed.

- Have a tasting session with chocolate, plain, milk and white. Which is their favourite?

- If you are making this recipe in the autumn or winter there may be fresh walnuts in the shops. Buy some so you can crack them open with children. The shells are beautifully textured and can be used to make small boats, models of tortoises or used in imaginary play.

- If they are carefully split open, the nut can be removed and the shells glued together again with a button or grains of rice inside to make intriguing little rattles.

### TEACHING POINTS

**Communication, Language and Literacy**
Use talk to organise, sequence and clarify thinking, ideas, feelings and events
Extend their vocabulary

**Knowledge and Understanding of the World**
Look closely at similarities and differences, patterns and change
Ask questions about why things happen and how things work

**Physical Development**
Handle tools with control

### What have children learned?

Can children predict what will happen to the butter and chocolate when it is heated? Do they use the word 'melt'?

Do they notice that the crumbs get smaller and smaller? Do they use the word 'smaller' (not 'littler'!)

Can older children suggest ways in which they could test if the cake has set?

Explain that the chocolate was hard/solid when they started, then it melted and eventually it became solid when it cooled.

### Involving parents

Copy out the recipe for parents so they can share the experience at home.

# Birthday cake

**Ingredients for sponge**
3 large eggs
85g caster sugar
85g plain flour
extra caster sugar

**Filling and icing ingredients**
4 tbsp strawberry or apricot jam
70g icing sugar for glace icing or 100g dark chocolate and 30g butter if making chocolate glaze

**Equipment**
electric hand mixer
mixing bowl
spoons
greaseproof paper
sieve
small basin for icing or glaze
saucepan
knife
swiss roll tin, greased and lined
clean tea towel to roll sponge
serving plate or board
cake decorations/candle holders and candles

**Oven:** 200°C/400°F/Gas 6

**Preparation time:** 40 minutes

**Cooking time:** 12-15 minutes

**Total time:** 1 hour plus decorating time once cake is cool

This is a simple birthday cake based on a swiss roll. It is essential to have an electric hand mixer if you want the sponge to be really light. Children will enjoy watching the eggs and sugar increase in volume but will not be able to have an active part until the sponge is out of the oven when they can help roll it up and then fill and decorate it.

## Method

Break the eggs into a mixing bowl, add the sugar and start whisking on a slow speed, gradually increasing the speed until the mixture is very pale and greatly increased in volume.

Sieve the flour into the bowl and fold into the mixture with a metal spoon, being very gentle.

Pour into the prepared tin and bake for about 12 to 15 minutes.

Dampen the tea towel. Lay out flat on the surface with the greaseproof paper on top of it. Sprinkle with a little caster sugar and tip the sponge out onto it.

With the help of the children roll the sponge up, using the paper to help you. Leave it on the cloth to cool.

While this is happening, make the glace icing or chocolate glaze. Mix the sieved icing sugar with enough water to make a thin pouring cream or place the chopped chocolate and butter in a basin and melt over a pan of hot water.

Carefully unroll the cooled cake and spread with jam. Re-roll and place on serving plate.

Coat with glace icing or chocolate, and arrange the decorations and candles on top.

Eat soon! As this cake has no fat it will not keep for more than a few hours.

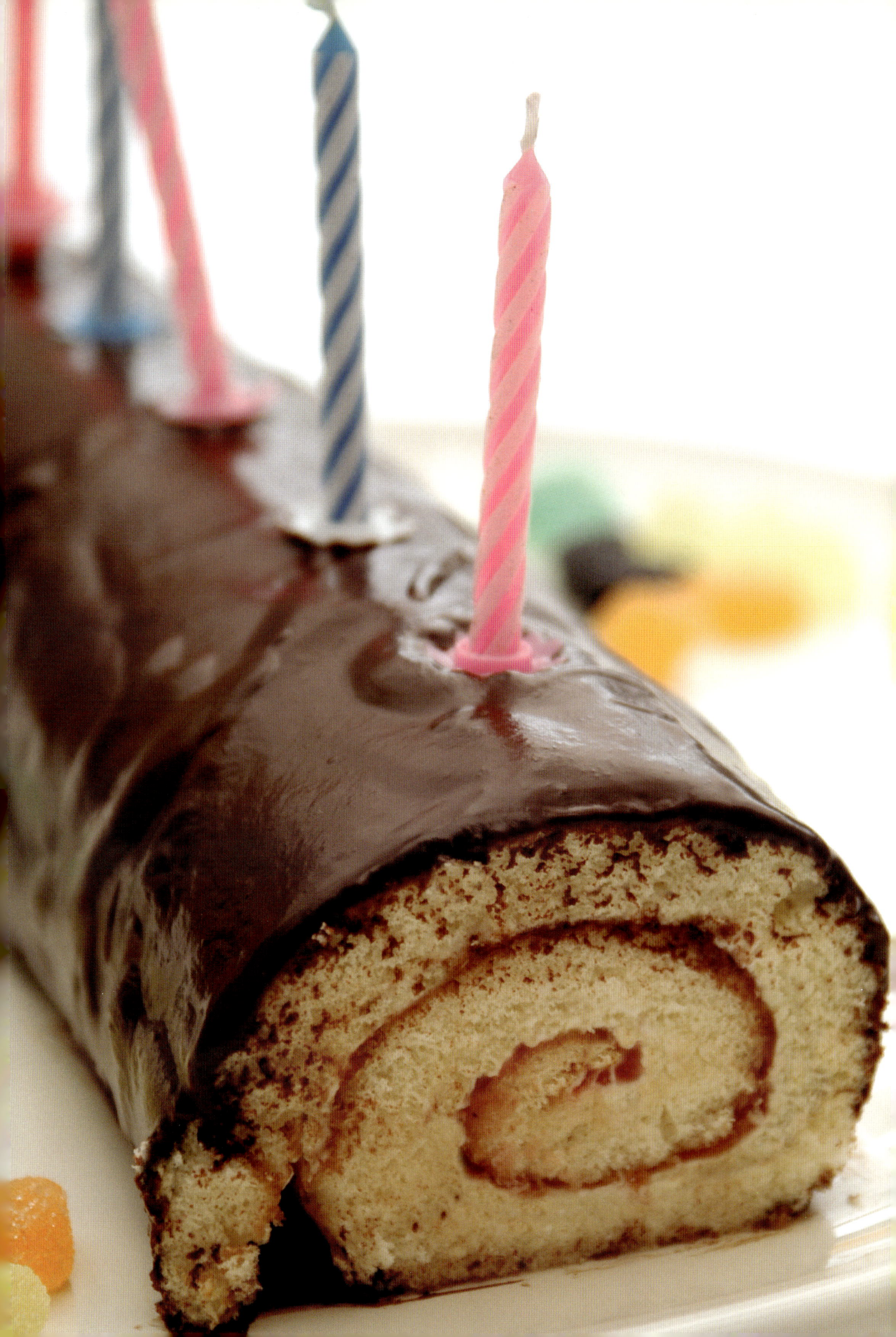

## Learning points

**Words you can use**: whisk, pale, sieve, roll, rectangle, spiral

Children will be able to see the changes to the colour and texture of the mixture as the air is beaten into the eggs and sugar.

Tell them that the flour must be mixed in very gently so the air is kept in the mixture.

Talk about the rectangular shape of the tin. Ask children what shape they think the finished cake will be.

The dampened tea towel helps to keep the cake soft and easy to roll. It is important to roll the cake while it is still warm.

Tell children that you are going to change the shape of the cake. If they stand at the side they will be able to see a spiral shape forming as you roll the cake.

If you are making glace icing, children can sieve the lumps out of the icing sugar. Be careful to add small drops of water until you have the right consistency - it is all too easy to end up with an over runny mixture. If you are making a chocolate glaze, let children watch the chocolate and butter melt.

Let children choose how to decorate the top of the cake

## Ideas for activities

- Provide playdough for children to roll out rectangles and then roll them into swiss roll shapes.

- Let children practise whisking with a rotary and a balloon whisk in a bowl of water. A few drops of washing-up liquid will create a mass of bubbles!

- Look for spirals: a slinky, mattress springs, spiral staircases, spiral shaped pasta, the thread on a screw, corkscrew.

## TEACHING POINTS

**Communication, Language and Literacy**
Use talk to organise, sequence and clarify thinking, ideas, feelings and events

Extend their vocabulary

**Mathematical Development**
Use language to describe the shape and size of solids and flat shapes

**Knowledge and Understanding of the World**
Look closely at similarities and differences, patterns and change

Ask questions about why things happen and how things work

**Physical Development**
Handle tools with increasing control

## What have children learned?

Do children notice the changes in the beaten egg mixture or the glaze?

Can they name the shape of the tin?

Do they recognise the spiral shape in the finished cake?

### Action rhyme

| | |
|---|---|
| My birthday cake is very good | (*Rub tummy*) |
| And round as it can be | (*Make a circle in the air*) |
| With icing on the top | (*Flat hand smoothing in a circle*) |
| And candles lit for me | (*Hold up fingers*) |
| I'll blow all the candles out | (*Blow*) |
| And we'll have cake for tea | (*Mime giving out slices of cake and eating*) |

Chris Heald

# Flapjacks

**Ingredients**
160g butter
160g soft brown sugar
2 tbsp golden syrup
350g rolled oats
pinch of salt

**Ingredients that could be added to mix with oats:**
50g peanuts and 50g raisins
60g plain chocolate chips

**Equipment**
saucepan
basin
knife
mixing spoons
baking tin 20 x 25cm, or 22cm square

**Oven:** 160°C/325°F/Gas 3

**Preparation time:**
10 minutes

**Cooking time:**
30–35 minutes

**Cooling time:** 10 minutes

Flapjacks are so well known they hardly need any introduction! The ingredients will be easy to find in any small local shop. They are quick and simple to cook and you can get on with other things while you are waiting for them to cool. You can add a variety of ingredients, such as nuts and raisins or chocolate chips, to ring the changes.

## Method

Melt the butter, sugar and syrup together in the saucepan without letting it become too warm.

Mix in the oats and salt then press into a greased tin. Bake for 30-35 minutes.

Leave to cool for 10 minutes and then cut into squares or oblongs, but leave to cool completely before removing from tin.

## Learning points

**Words you can use**: melt, square, rectangle. For older children: solid, liquid

Ask children to predict what they think will happen to the butter as it is heated. Here is another chance for children to understand how some ingredients melt when heated. As heat is applied to the sugar it dissolves into the butter. This is a difficult concept for young children to understand. Don't worry if they say the sugar is melting, too.

Help children to talk about how the mixture changes when the oats are added.

Ask children if they would like the flapjacks cut into squares or rectangles.

## Ideas for activities

- If you are making flapjacks in late summer or early autumn you may be able to gather a few stalks of a cereal crop to show children what oats, barley and wheat look like.

- Place some grains of a cereal crop in a pestle and mortar or under a rolling pin so that children can see what happens to the seeds as they are crushed into flour.

## TEACHING POINTS

**Communication, Language and Literacy**
Use talk to organise, sequence and clarify thinking, ideas, feelings and events

Extend their vocabulary

**Knowledge and Understanding of the World**
Look closely at similarities and differences, patterns and change

Ask questions about why things happen and how things work

### What have children learned?

Do they notice the changes in the butter?

Do they use the word 'melt'?

Can they press the mixture into the tin?

**Older children:**
Can they recognise that the butter has changed from a solid to a liquid? They may not be able to use these exact words but may say 'the butter was hard and now it's runny'.

Are they able to describe the difference between a square and a rectangle?

# Cheese biscuits

**Ingredients**
150g plain flour
100g butter
120g strong cheddar cheese or a mixture of cheddar and fresh Parmesan
1/2 tsp salt
1/2 tsp Dijon mustard
1 egg yolk mixed with 1 tbsp milk
2 tbsp sesame seeds

**Equipment**
large and small mixing bowls
blunt knife and fork
small bowl or cup
cheese grater
baking trays, greased

**Oven:** 375°F/190°C/Gas 5

**Preparation time:** 15-20 minutes

**Cooking time:** 12-18 minutes

This recipe needs children to be deft with their hands and so it's good for physical development. They will need to crumble, roll and flatten using just the right amount of pressure. The biscuits are delicious!

## Method

Grate the cheese on the smaller holes of the grater, showing children how to do this without hurting their fingers.

Place the flour in a bowl, add the butter and cut into small pieces. Rub the butter into the flour using the fingertips and explain how this has to be done with light, quick movements, so that the butter does not become too warm and stick to the fingers. When it looks like breadcrumbs, add the cheese to the bowl.

Mix the salt, mustard, egg yolk and milk together in a small bowl and stir into the flour. Mix with a fork until it comes together, then gather it into a ball with the fingers.

Break off lumps the size of a small walnut and let children roll these into balls. Sprinkle the sesame seeds onto the work surface and roll the balls into them so they are coated all over.

Place on a greased baking tray and flatten the balls with the heel of the hand – but not too hard.

Bake for 12 to 18 minutes until golden. Leave to cool for 2 or 3 minutes, but remove from tray before they become too crisp or they might crumble and break.

## Learning points

**Words you can use**: grate, rub, fingertips, breadcrumbs, heel of hand

Be sure that children have a safe grip of the cheese when grating. You may prefer to do the grating towards the end to make sure children do not hurt their hands.

If children have crumbled stale bread for the birds this technique of mixing butter and flour will be easy. The flour sticks to the butter and in turn the hands separate the butter into smaller pieces until the mixture looks like breadcrumbs.

Children love rolling mixture into balls. Ask them how they think the sesame seeds stick without any glue.

Remind children they have a heel to their foot and now show them the heel of the hand. Too much pressure on the mixture from the heel of the hand will make it difficult to lift the cooked biscuits off the tray.

### TEACHING POINTS

**Communication, Language and Literacy**
Use talk to organise, sequence and clarify thinking, ideas, feelings and events

Extend their vocabulary

**Mathematical Development**
Use language much as 'more', 'less', 'bigger', 'smaller'

**Knowledge and Understanding of the World**
Look closely at similarities and differences, patterns and change

**Physical Development**
Move with control and coordination

### What have children learned?

Are children able to coordinate their thumbs and fingers to crumble the mixture?

Can they remember the position for the heel of the hand and the fingertips?

### Involving parents

In winter months (only) ask parents to save stale bread for the birds. This can be made into fine breadcrumbs by practising the same physical skills as in this recipe.

# Shortbread biscuits

**Ingredients**
150g butter (left at room temperature to soften)
200g plain flour
50g cornflour plus a little extra for dipping
50g caster sugar

**Equipment**
mixing bowl
forks
wooden spoons
large baking tray, greased
electric hand mixer if available

**For rounds:**
rolling pin
cutters

**Oven:** 325°F/165°C/Gas 3

**Preparation time:**
20-30 minutes mixing and shaping

30 minutes resting

**Cooking time:** 12-15 minutes

Shortbread biscuits are traditional Scottish fare. They could be made and eaten on Burns' night (25 January).

## Method

Place the softened butter in a bowl with the sugar. Cream together using a wooden spoon or the mixer on a slow speed. When the mixture is light and fluffy, start adding the flour and cornflour a spoonful at a time. Work until all the flour is incorporated. Wrap the mixture in cling-film and leave to rest in the refrigerator or a cool place for 30 minutes or longer if more convenient.

Divide the dough into small lumps about the size of a large cherry. To make fingers, show children how to roll each piece into a short sausage shape and place on the baking tray with spaces between each one.

Dip the fork into the cornflour and lightly press on each biscuit to give a ridged effect, without squashing it flat!

For shortbread rounds, lightly roll the dough and cut into small circles.

Bake for 12 to 15 minutes. Cool a little, and then loosen from the tray and leave to cool completely before eating or storing in an airtight tin.

## Learning points

**Words you can use**: cream, light, fluffy, rest, press, same size

Creaming butter and sugar together is a common method for biscuit and cake making. Make sure that children notice the changes in colour and texture from the start to the end of the mixing when it becomes light and fluffy. The mixture changes again when the flour is added. Let children have a chance to stir so they can feel the change.

Most children will be able to roll a sausage shape. Make sure they are not too long. You could use this opportunity to measure and compare so that the sausages are roughly the same size. Count how many you have. If children are keeping their own biscuits, ask them how many they think they will each have.

You will need to make sure that children do not press so enthusiastically that their biscuit stays glued to the tray! Help them to see the pattern that emerges as the dough is forced between the tines of the fork.

When the biscuits are baked, ask children what changes might have happened to the biscuits while they were in the oven. Encourage them to use words such as 'hard', 'crisp', 'hot', 'darker'.

## Ideas for activities

- Give children forks of varying sizes with their playdough so that they can use them to make patterns. You could also find some toys and kitchen equipment for them to experiment with pressing. For toys, try Stickle bricks or Duplo. For kitchen equipment, try a garlic press, colander or sieve.

## TEACHING POINTS

**Communication, Language and Literacy**
Use talk to organise, sequence and clarify thinking, ideas, feelings and events
Extend their vocabulary

**Mathematical Development**
Use mathematical language such as 'longer', 'shorter', 'same as'
Say and use number names

**Knowledge and Understanding of the World**
Look closely at similarities and differences, patterns and change
Ask why things happen and how things work

## What have children learned?

Do children notice changes in the mixture at different stages?

Can they count accurately and compare their dough sausages with others?

Can they use words and phrases such as 'longer', 'shorter', 'same as'?

Do they have the skill to roll a sausage shape smoothly?

## Involving parents

Make some playdough (see page 52) and divide into lumps, filling a small margarine tub that children can take home to play with.

# Gingerbread men

These fancy spiced biscuits go back centuries in Britain when they were sold at street markets and fairs. They are said to be the oldest cake-bread in the world, reputedly invented by a Greek baker. Any children who have been to Greece may have seen fancy spiced cakes and cookies in special baker's shops. They have changed over the ages and gingerbread men are now more biscuit than bread. Of course, children can make gingerbread women or children or any shape that fires the imagination. Decoration may be simple, such as currants for eyes and buttons or, if time allows, for special occasions decorate with icing and almonds.

### Ingredients
80g butter
80g golden syrup or clear honey
100g sugar
1 tsp ground ginger
350g self-raising flour
1 tsp bicarbonate of soda
pinch cinnamon
1 egg, beaten
25g currants

### Optional icing
75g icing sugar
1 tsp lemon juice or more if needed
8 whole blanched almonds or currants

### Equipment
small saucepan
mixing bowl
rolling pin
wooden spoon
gingerbread people cutters or other shapes - children could make their own stencils from polystyrene sheets or thick card
baking tray(s) lightly greased

**Oven:** 350°F/180°C/Gas 4

**Preparation time:** 30 minutes

**Cooking time:** 15 minutes

## Method

Stir butter and syrup or honey in a small pan until blended. Do not allow to become too hot. Add spices and allow to cool a little.

Mix the flour, bicarbonate and sugar together in a bowl.

Add the mix from the saucepan together with the beaten egg. Stir and knead until smooth. Leave to cool for 10 minutes.

Roll out on a floured surface and cut into shapes.

Lay on lightly greased baking trays. Put in eyes and buttons.

Bake for 10-15 minutes until golden and set.

If using icing instead of currants, mix the icing sugar, lemon juice and teaspoon of hot water until smooth and spread on warm men and decorate as desired.

## Learning points

**Words you can use:** spices, sieve, roll, thin, thick, eyes, nose, mouth, buttons

As the golden syrup is heated it will become more runny. Ask children to notice the change. Do they smell the spicy aroma as the mixture is warmed?

When sieving the flour, notice if there are any lumps and occasionally hold the sieve high so children can see the flour falling through. This also adds more air to the mixture.

The mixture will start to feel stiffer as the flour is mixed with the other ingredients. Can the children feel the difference?

Make sure the work surface and rolling pin are well floured to prevent the mixture from sticking. Ask children what is happening to the mixture as it is rolled. Introduce words such as 'thick', 'thin', 'flat', 'smooth', 'larger', 'smaller'. If children have made their own stencils they will need to trace around them with a knife.

What are the different shapes and sizes of gingerbread men?

### TEACHING POINTS

**Communication language and Literacy**
Use talk to organise, sequence and clarify thinking, ideas, feelings and events

Retell narratives, drawing on the language patterns of stories

Extend their vocabulary

**Mathematical Development**
Say and use number names, counting to ten

Use language such as 'more', 'less', 'circle', 'bigger', 'smaller'

**Knowledge and Understanding of the World**
Investigate objects and materials by using all their senses as appropriate

Look closely at similarities and differences, patterns and change

Ask questions about why things happen and how things work

**Physical Development**
Handle tools with increasing control

**Creative Development**
Sing simple songs from memory

Decide what will help you to measure the cooking time – a clock, kitchen timer, watch, sand timer? Help children to recognise when the time will be up and the gingerbread cooked.

When decorating the gingerbread men there will be opportunities for counting facial features such as eyes and buttons. Do all the children have the same number of buttons?

When placing the gingerbread men on the tray, notice how soft and floppy the dough appears to be.

See how many men you can place on one baking sheet. Will some gingerbread men have to lie upside down to fit on the tray? Whose gingerbread man lies close to the edge? Whose lies in the middle of the tray? Are the gingerbread men lying in order of size?

When the gingerbread men have cooled, draw children's attention to how the dough has changed to become firm, yet brittle.

## Ideas for activities

- Act out the story of 'The gingerbread man' using a simple glove puppet made from felt or small world toys and animals.

- Make some playdough and use cutters for the characters in the story.

## TEACHING POINTS

### What have children learned?

Can children count the number of currants they have used?

Can they compare the different features of the gingerbread men?

Do they notice the various changes in the mixture?

Can they repeat the rhyme 'Run, run, as fast as you can, you can't catch me I'm the gingerbread man'?

### Involving parents

Copy the recipe so that children can make gingerbread men with their parents at home.

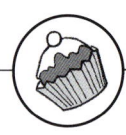

# Fairy cakes

**Ingredients**
120g soft butter
100g caster sugar
2 eggs, beaten
120g self-raising flour

optional extras - finely grated zest of a lemon/1tbsp cocoa to replace 1tbsp flour/1tbsp sultanas

60g icing sugar if you wish to ice the cakes

**Equipment**
mixing bowl
wooden spoons
dessertspoons
small bowl
bun tins and paper cases to line them with

**Oven:** 350°F/180°C/Gas 4

**Preparation time:**
20-30 minutes

**Cooking time:**
15- 20 minutes

No recipe book for children would be complete without a recipe for small cakes. It is easy to change the flavour of the cakes with any of the optional ingredients. You can also add variety by offering a range of decorations, such as chocolate hundreds and thousands.

## Method

Place all the ingredients in a mixing bowl and begin to mix gently.

Place the paper cases in the bun trays and put dessertspoonfuls in each one.

Place in pre-heated oven and bake for 15 minutes or until firm to touch.

Leave to cool. The cakes may be iced with a simple glace icing. Mix 60g sieved icing sugar with a dessertspoon of water or lemon juice, adding a little more liquid if necessary until it is a smooth cream, and spoon a little on each cake.

## Learning points

**Words you can use**: egg, yolk, stir, spoonful, icing, change, pattern

At first, the ingredients will be easy to identify. Ask children what they think will happen to the ingredients as they start to stir. Do they know that the yolks will break? Let each child have a go at stirring the mixture. Ask them what the mixture looks like at the end. How has it changed?

Count the spaces in the bun tray. Ask them to see a pattern in the tray; a common pattern is four rows of three. Ask children how many paper cases they will need to fill the tray and let them count them out. Each child should have a turn at spooning out some of the mixture. Did they need all the cases? Do they need another tray?

As the cakes are placed in the oven, ask what children think they will look like when they are cooked.

You will not need much liquid to make the icing. If you add too much then just add a little more icing sugar to make the mixture thicker. Be sure to get children to see the changes that take place.

## Ideas for activities

- Let children have a bun tray and some paper cases to use in imaginary play to give them the chance to practise matching and counting.

- Read *A Bun for Barney* by Joyce Dunbar and illustrated by Emilie Boon (Orchard Books). Barney is a bear with a five cherried bun. This story gives you opportunities for talking about subtraction.

## TEACHING POINTS

**Communication, Language and Literacy**
Use talk to organise, sequence and clarify thinking, ideas, feelings and events
Extend their vocabulary

**Mathematical Development**
Say and use number names

**Knowledge and Understanding of the World**
Look closely at similarities and differences, patterns and change
Ask questions about why things happen and how things work

### What have children learned?
Are children able to predict in simple ways what will happen as the mixture is stirred?
Can they match the bun cases to the spaces in the bun tray?
Can they count using one-to-one correspondence? If so, how far?
Do they notice the pattern in the bun tray, for example three rows of four?

### Involving parents
If the cakes are to be taken home, ask parents to talk to their children about who will eat them and how they might be shared.

COOK AND LEARN TOGETHER

# Mini Christmas cakes

## Ingredients
120g soft butter
80g soft brown sugar
180g self-raising flour
2 large eggs, lightly beaten
330g good quality fruit mincemeat
zest and juice of half a lemon
dried fruit and nuts - 50g chopped almonds, 50g glace cherries, 50g raisins (optional)

## Decoration
350g white marzipan
ready to roll coloured icing (about 350g)
2 tbsp apricot jam
icing sugar
selection of decorations such as silver or coloured balls, sweets, hundreds and thousands, ready made cake decorations such as snowmen or Christmas trees

## Equipment
6 small baked bean tins, washed and dried, making sure there are no sharp edges
mixing bowl
wooden and metal spoons
greaseproof paper
baking tray
board for rolling marzipan and icing
rolling pins
pastry brush
small bowls or cups
tin foil for storing

**Oven:** 325°F/170°C/Gas 3

**Preparation time:**
30–40 minutes

**Cooking time:** about 30 minutes

These cakes are easy to make and will store well for a short time. They could be made early in the autumn and placed in the freezer before the final decoration near Christmas. Decorating the cakes gives children an opportunity to be creative and use their own ideas of celebration.

## Method
Prepare the tins by brushing well with melted lard or butter and placing discs of greaseproof paper on the base. Grease again and set aside.

Place all the ingredients, apart from the mincemeat, in a mixing bowl and mix gently with a wooden spoon. Then beat the mixture until it is smooth. Add the mincemeat and the extra fruit and nuts if desired.

Using a dessertspoon, put the mixture in the tins. This might be rather messy!

Place the tins on a baking tray and put in the oven for about 30 minutes. Test with a skewer or similar to check they are cooked in the middle. (If the skewer comes out cleanly then the cake is cooked.) If necessary, return to the oven for a few more minutes. Cool and then carefully remove from tins.

Wrap each cake in tin foil and store in a cool place for up to seven days or freeze.

When ready to decorate, unwrap and place each cake on a small cake board or improvise with cardboard and foil. Brush the tops with apricot jam. If the jam is stiff, place a few spoons in a saucepan and warm gently on the hob. It will then spread much more easily.

Roll the marzipan out on a board dusted with icing sugar to 5mm thickness and cut circles to fit the tops using the bean tins as templates. Place on the cakes and press to fit.

Roll out the icing to fit the top of the marzipan and let the children decorate to their hearts content.

Leave to dry and then wrap in cellophane and tie with ribbons to make seasonal gifts.

## Learning points

**Words you can use:** circle, mincemeat, roll, marzipan, icing, decoration

Greasing tins prevents the mixture from sticking to them. The greaseproof paper gives added protection to the cakes. Using a tin as a template to draw round means that the paper should fit the size of tin. Give children plenty of time for this part.

There will be many chances to talk about numbers as children weigh out the ingredients on the scales. Ask them what they notice as the ingredients are mixed together.

Ask children to count the number of spoons they use to fill their tin.

Count the number of tins and the number of people cooking. Is there one for everyone?

See if children can work out the amount of tin foil they will need to wrap their cake.

The jam is the glue to keep the marzipan in place! Ask children why jam is good glue for cakes.

Ask them what shape they will need to cover the top of their cake. This is a good opportunity to talk about shapes.

After the icing has been placed on top of the marzipan, let children choose from a range of decorative materials. Talk about colour, size and shape as they make their choices.

## Ideas for activities

- Use different-sized tins to draw round and make a pattern of overlapping circles.

- Make a model of a Christmas cake for children to use in their imaginary play.

- Put out playdough, rolling pins and decorative materials to make playdough cakes.

### TEACHING POINTS

**Mathematical Development**
Use developing mathematical ideas to solve practical problems

**Knowledge and Understanding of the World**
Look closely at similarities and differences, patterns and change

Ask questions about why things happen and how things work

**Creative Development**
Use their imagination in art and design

Explore colour, texture, shape and form in two and three dimensions

### What have children learned?

Are children able to identify a circle and recognise that drawing around a tin will give them a circular piece of paper?

Can they recognise any numbers on the scales?

Are they able to count accurately the number of spoons of mixture?

Do they make choices and express their individuality in decorating their cake?

### Involving parents

Ask parents to collect baked bean tins for the cake moulds and to let their children explore a range of tins of different sizes from the kitchen cupboard.

# Picnics and no-cook food

There are many things you can prepare to eat which do not need a cooker. For some, though, a kettle or other means of boiling water are required. Sandwiches are ideal no-cook food as they can be wonderfully varied, sweet or savoury.

### Sandwiches

Here are some ideas for sandwich fillings, which are easy to make:

Grated cheese mixed with softened butter - add raisins as an optional extra
Flaked tinned tuna mixed with mayonnaise and sliced cucumber
Chopped hard-boiled egg with skinned sliced tomato
Grated apple and chopped dates, with a little lemon juice
Mashed banana with grated carrot

The sandwiches can be cut into a variety of shapes. Biscuit and tart cutters can be useful.

# Hummus bi tahini

**Ingredients**
400g can of chick peas
2 peeled cloves of garlic
juice of 2 to 3 lemons (depending on size)
2 or 3 tbsp tahini or more to taste
salt
1 to 2 tbsp olive oil
1/2 tsp paprika (optional)

**Equipment**
dessertspoon
lemon juicer
can opener
2 basins or plastic containers
sieve
flat bladed knife or garlic press
fork
chopping board

**Preparation time:** 15 to 25 minutes

This chick pea and tahini dip, widely eaten in the Middle East, is quick to make, tasty and nourishing. It's usually made in a processor or blender, but you can make it by hand - it just gives a rougher texture. Tahini is a puree of sesame seeds. It is usually sold in jars and can be bought in most large supermarkets or delicatessens. Sticks of raw vegetables (crudités), pitta bread or tortilla chips all go well with it.

## Method

Open the can of chick peas. Drain them through a sieve, keeping some of the liquid in case it is needed to loosen the paste.

Crush the garlic cloves with a little salt using the back of a flat-bladed knife on the board or a garlic press. Put the garlic in a bowl.

Place the sieve on top of the same bowl and push the chick peas through with a wooden spoon. If any of the chick peas will not go through, tip them into the basin and crush with a fork.

Beat together with a wooden spoon, adding the tahini and lemon juice gradually. If the mixture seems too thick, add some of the reserved liquid and beat vigorously. The children will enjoy this, but make sure you are holding the bowl firmly!

Taste and adjust seasoning, beating in a little of the oil, and sprinkle a little paprika on the top.

COOK AND LEARN TOGETHER

## Learning points

**Words you can use**: drain, sieve, press, push, crush

Before tipping the chick peas into the sieve, ask children what they think will happen. What might happen if the holes in the sieve were very big? Would the chick peas fall through?

Garlic has a pungent smell. Does it remind the children of onions?

When the chick peas are crushed and pushed through the sieve, draw children's attention to the changes. Ask them what it feels like as they rub the sieve with the wooden spoon.

There is another chance to see how substances change when new ingredients are added. Do children think the mixture is getting stiffer and harder to stir or thinner and easier to stir?

Salt brings out the full flavour of food. Paprika, which is made from dried red peppers, adds visual interest to the bland appearance of the dip.

## Ideas for activities

- Give children a range of utensils and containers with holes to play with in sand or water: a flour sifter, colanders, sieves of varying sizes, together with some pea-sized objects, for example dried chick peas, pebbles, acorns, beads. They can then repeat or act out some of the stages in the recipe.

- Provide colanders, sieves, a garlic press and other utensils with playdough so that children can push the dough through the holes.

- Under careful supervision, let children experiment with mixing different substances so that they can see the changes that take place. Collect oil, water, bicarbonate of soda, lemon juice or vinegar, talcum powder, salt and sugar. Use some shallow plastic dishes or a paint palette in which to mix two ingredients. Try the following combinations:

- Water with talc or oil;

- Lemon juice or vinegar with bicarbonate of soda;

- Water with salt or sugar.

## TEACHING POINTS

**Communication, Language and Literacy**
Use talk to organise, sequence and clarify thinking, ideas, feelings and events

Extend their vocabulary

**Knowledge and Understanding of the World**
Look closely at similarities and differences, patterns and change

Ask questions about why things happen and how things work

Select tools and techniques they need to shape the materials they are using

### What have children learned?

Have children the physical strength to crush the garlic and chick peas, to stir and beat the ingredients?

Do they notice the changes to the garlic and chick peas as they change from solids into a puree?

What happens when the lemon juice and oil are added?

### Involving parents

Encourage parents to give children sieves and colanders to use at bath time or outside in the paddling pool.

# Marzipan sweets

## Ingredients
300g-500g marzipan
food colourings (as many as affordable)
icing sugar
flaked almonds, walnuts and chocolate drops if desired

## Equipment
pastry boards or bakewell paper
blunt knives
small bowls to mix colouring and marzipan
sweet paper cases if desired

**Preparation time:** at least 30 minutes (plus 30 minutes for the marzipan to dry)

## Warning
This recipe contains nuts so should not be used if there is any possibility of a child having a nut allergy.

Although homemade marzipan is tastier and healthier, containing less sugar than commercially available marzipan, it is probably much easier to buy it at the supermarket or health food store. Children should be able to make various shapes and will enjoy using the different colours and making their own individual decorations.

## Method

Make sure the marzipan is at room temperature and give each child some of it to roll.

Add a drop of colour to each portion and show children how to knead the mixture until the colour is even.

Sprinkle a little icing sugar on the surface to prevent stickiness.

Talk about the fillings and explain that for a large nut or fruit, they will have to break off a larger piece of marzipan to wrap around it. Show how to close and join the marzipan to hide the filling.

Leave on bakewell paper to dry at room temperature for 30 minutes and then put the sweets in the paper cases.

## Learning points

**Words you can use**: marzipan, sticky, roll, knead, icing sugar

Explain to children that the warmth of their hands will soften the marzipan so that they can easily shape it.

Ask them to watch carefully as they knead the colouring into the marzipan. Can they see swirls of colour as it mixes?

Icing sugar, like flour, prevents ingredients from sticking. Ask children what it feels like to have the icing sugar on their hands.

Discuss whether they want a hard centre (nut) or a soft centre (fruit) for their sweets.

The warmth of their hands made the marzipan malleable. Now the sweets need to dry in the air.

Can children count how many they have made and work out how many sweet cases they will need?

## Ideas for activities

- Are there any other sweets that children could make? Peppermint creams are a favourite and need no cooking.

- Make some pretend sweets together to play with – use playdough with beads for the filling.

- Sweets are nice but too many are not good for us - talk about why it's important to have a healthy diet and to look after your teeth.

## TEACHING POINTS

**Mathematical Development**

Say number names, counting to ten

Use language such as 'more', 'less', 'circle', 'bigger', 'smaller'

**Knowledge and Understanding of the World**

Investigate by using all their senses

Look closely at similarities and differences, patterns and change

Ask questions about why things happen and how things work

**Physical Development**

Handle malleable materials with increasing control

## What have children learned?

Can they count up to ten? Up to 20?

Can they match the number of sweets to cases?

Are they able to use their fingers well to roll, knead and enclose a filling?

Are they able to talk about the feeling on their hands when the mixture becomes too sticky?

## Involving parents

Tell parents that you have been talking about dental care. Ask children about when they brush their teeth, the colour of their toothbrush, the toothpaste they use.

# Chocolate fruit and nut clusters

### Ingredients
100g dark or milk chocolate
1 tbsp chopped almonds
1 tbsp hazelnuts, whole or chopped
1 tbsp walnut quarters
1 tbsp raisins
1 tbsp sultanas
1 tbsp pumpkin seeds
1 tbsp sunflower seeds
Any combination of nuts and seeds may be used
Strawberries or raspberries may be used in season (but will not keep)

### Equipment
small basin
small saucepan
16 small foil or paper cups (3 cm diameter by 2 cm deep)
teaspoons

**Preparation time:**
15 minutes

**Setting time:** 1 hour

These treats are fun to make for a festival or for presents for children to give at Christmas. Children love to choose their own assortment of nuts, seeds or fruits. If using fresh fruit such as strawberries or cherries, the chocolates would have to be eaten the same day. With dried fruit and nuts they can be kept refrigerated in a covered container for up to two weeks.

### Method
Break the chocolate into small pieces and put into a basin. Place some water in a saucepan and bring to the boil. Remove from heat and place the basin over the hot water and leave to melt. (If a microwave oven is available, the chocolate may be melted on low power for a short time. Take care not to overheat as the chocolate will become unworkable.)

Divide the melted chocolate among the cups, filling them to about 5 mm depth.

Now let children put pieces of fruit and nuts into the chocolate, making their own choices and pressing in enough to make sure they stick in the chocolate. Refrigerate or leave in a cool place to set for an hour.

## Learning points

**Words you can use**: melt, hot, warm, cool, set, names of some seeds such as pumpkin and sunflower, nuts

Tell children that you need to melt the chocolate. Explain that you are using a basin because you do not want the mixture to get too hot. If possible, help them watch the melting process. Get them to compare the chocolate at the beginning of the recipe and in its melted state. Do they think the taste of the chocolate will have changed?

Children will see the chocolate in its liquid form as it is poured into the cups. Ask them what they think will happen as it becomes cooler.

This is the time for children to choose how they will decorate their chocolate cup. If you are using dried seeds and nuts, draw their attention to the similarities and differences between the ingredients.

## Ideas for activities

- Keep a few seeds and nuts to look at. If you have a large magnifying glass, encourage children to see the small details.
- In the autumn, go for a walk in a wooded area to look for nuts, seeds and berries from wild plants. Be sure to explain that these seeds would not be good to eat and that some berries can make you very ill, so they should only pick them when an adult is with them.

## TEACHING POINTS

**Communication, Language and Literacy**
Use talk to organise, sequence and clarify thinking, ideas, feelings and events
Extend their vocabulary

**Knowledge and Understanding of the World**
Look closely at similarities and differences, patterns and change
Ask questions about why things happen and how things work

**Creative Development**
Explore colour, texture, shape and form

### What have children learned?
Can children predict what will happen to the chocolate when it is heated? Do they use the word 'melt'? They may be able to think of a hot day when they have eaten chocolate!
Are older children able to explain that the chocolate was hard/solid when they started, then it melted and eventually it became solid when it cooled?

### Involving parents
Copy out the recipe for parents so they can make some more of these simple gifts for the family.

# How cooking helps children learn

## Personal, Social and Emotional Development

**Successful personal, social and emotional development is vital for very young children. It is the foundation for everything they do.**

### Attitudes to learning

We want children to be interested, excited and motivated. Their eagerness to try new activities, along with their natural curiosity about the world around them, are vital skills for lifelong learning. If children are to grow up feeling positive and confident in themselves, they need experiences that are enjoyable and that give them the chance to be in control and successful. Cooking or preparing food can include all of this.

Children's attitudes are formed early, particularly over food. By introducing them to a wide range of foods you will be encouraging varied diets and healthier lives.

Provide plenty of opportunities for children to be involved. Although many baking recipes suggest using one big bowl, you could share the mixture between four smaller bowls to give children more responsibility and independence.

Encourage children to measure out ingredients for themselves and work out solutions to any problems they meet. For example, if they weigh out too much flour, how can they put some back in the bag? Allowing children to think about and to practise ways of solving problems fosters confidence. Of course, everyone should play their part in washing up!

### Customs and traditions

Learning more about their own culture helps children to develop a sense of belonging and a stronger sense of self-image. Acknowledging children's cultural food heritage makes each child and family feel valued. It fosters self-respect and respect for others.

Food and cooking have strong cultural links and sometimes may be of religious or historical significance. Just as there are strong differences there are also traditions that are shared. For instance, most cultures make some form of bread or use specific dishes to celebrate religious festivals.

For many centuries Britain has imported foods native to other countries. Radishes originated in China and jam making began in the Middle East and was brought to

### TEACHING POINTS

Snack time is a good chance for children to take responsibility for pouring out drinks and preparing and organising the distribution of food. Don't be afraid of spills, they can easily be mopped up – by the children, of course!

Even if all your children come from one culture, it is still important to provide a culturally varied diet – not only is it a more interesting way of eating, but it helps to guard against the feelings that the food we eat is better than anyone else's.

Think about the role-play opportunities you offer. Are children only able to cook English food? If so, introduce some diversity. You could add a wok and some chopsticks after you have explored Chinese food together.

Europe by the Crusaders. So many foods, which are thought typically British, have their origins elsewhere.

The ways in which each food is served and eaten can differ. In some cultures only the right hand is used to eat with. In others, chopsticks may be used and the bowl raised close to the mouth. In some cultures, mouths must be rinsed after eating. So you need to be aware of individual children's needs and customs.

## Working with others

Cooking and eating are wonderful ways for children to learn to take turns and work well together. Cooking is best done in small groups of about four children. That way, there can be plenty of involvement and work for everyone, and not too much time waiting.

For longer recipes, such as soup or bread making, different children could be involved at different stages of the preparation so that more children can be included, but sometimes children need to see the complete sequence of events.

Eating can be in a larger group. Sharing and eating food are traditional ways of helping people to feel part of a group and welcoming guests. It helps to build relationships, so it is good if you can join in, too. Sit with children to help model the social conventions of meal times, such as conversation. Some children may not have much experience of family meals.

Make the most of opportunities to encourage considerate behaviour while sharing food, for example only handling the food you will eat and not that of others and, of course, saying please and thank you.

## Finding out their feelings

Children need to become aware of their own needs, views and feelings. Most of these will be centred on daily activities and special events. Preparing and eating food gives them the chance to talk about their own likes and dislikes as well as helping them to be sensitive to what other people think.

Children's taste buds react more effectively than adults' so when a child says that they don't like something, try to understand just how strong that dislike might be.

You may have strong emotions associated with a particular food or meal. So vivid are these emotions that they can be triggered by the smell alone - boiling cabbage or the scent of warm chocolate may bring memories flooding back! The same goes for children too.

### TEACHING POINTS

Children may be more willing to try new food at their childcare setting or school than at home, raising the frequent cry from a parent that 'S/he never eats that at home!' It may simply be the powerful influence of other children that makes the difference. You may want to reassure the parent and ask them to congratulate their child on their eagerness to try new foods.

# Communication, Language and Literacy

You will find many opportunities to ask questions and encourage children to talk about what they are doing and what is happening. You can help them to remember the sequence of events in a recipe or ask them to predict what might happen next.

## Talking

Children love new words, especially long ones. Teaching them about food and cooking will naturally extend their vocabulary.

Use the correct name for all the ingredients, utensils and actions. Say 'dust with flour' or 'stir the yeast into the flour' not 'mix this with that'. Although children may understand what has to be done it helps to expand their collection of new words or expressions.

Cookery involves all the senses so it can be a truly multi-sensory experience.

**Sight:** Talk about what they see. What happens when liquids are mixed with dry ingredients, for instance, when eggs are stirred into butter and sugar? What do they notice about egg whites or cream as they are whisked? Watch how chocolate changes as it sets and how water freezes when it is made into ice-lollies. Look for the differences between sugar and salt and if you cannot see any, wonder if there might be another way of identifying them.

**Hearing:** Listen for the sounds such as the bubble-bubble-plop sound that soup makes as it boils, or the pop of popcorn as it is heated. Make up simple repetitive rhymes and chants to represent the sounds and action. These help children to play with rhythm and rhyme which, later, will help with reading.

**Smell:** There is nothing quite like the warm smell of baking or the indulgence of heated chocolate but there will be much more to explore. Herbs and spices are particularly aromatic.

**Taste:** When sampling food, encourage children to identify not just their likes and dislikes, but also whether things are sweet, sour or salty; hot, warm or cold; dry, juicy, chewy or slippery.

**Touch:** Ask children to describe the feel or appearance of raw dough. If they say 'funny', ask 'What sort of funny?' or 'Funny like ....?' When making soup or a salad, compare a sliced tomato with a carrot or cucumber. Watch as the children handle utensils and be ready to give help with how to hold the object and how much pressure to use.

## Reading

Children are far more likely to want to read if the words or tasks mean something to them. Reading a recipe is a useful way of finding out how to make something good to eat. As you trace your finger under the words, children will be learning that reading, in English, is done from left to right and

COOK AND LEARN TOGETHER

from the top of the page to the bottom. You can show them how the information is organised on the page: the ingredients section, the utensils section and the step-by-step method sequence of what to do.

As you read together, children may spot some letters of the alphabet which they recognise from their name.

There will be labels and writing on just about every packet of food that you buy. This is an excellent way of drawing children's attention to the use of pictures and labels for giving information. Such is the power of advertising that there will be some products that they recognise just from the colour and symbols used on the packaging.

Look for a range of books that have food or cookery as their theme. Children will soon see the difference between story and information books, but may find it a little more difficult to tell a general information book from a recipe book. Help them to become familiar with the numbering on the contents page and the alphabetically ordered index.

When reading picture books, take the opportunity to talk about the title and the name of the author and illustrator. Older children may be interested to know about bar codes, publishers, price and the cover blurb that tells you a bit about the book.

There are many information and picture books and rhymes to do with food. These will help to reinforce learning and perhaps give an extra dimension. The story of the Little Red Hen, for instance, helps children to understand that we may all play a part in hard work to reap the benefit later.

## Writing

There are many ways to introduce writing as part of a cookery session. Name labels can be written on a brown paper bag for carrying the food home or beside the product. Younger children may only be able to make letter-like marks to represent their name. Older children can be encouraged to write their first name and family name.

Labels such as 'hot' or 'Please do not touch' help children to understand written warnings or instructions.

Single words or short phrases can be used in a play area: 'open' and 'closed' labels for cafes, menus for take-away restaurants, shopping lists for trips to the supermarket, preparation tasks for a party and posters for the baker's shop.

Making captions for books or pictures with children gives you the chance to show that there needs to be a capital letter at the beginning of a caption and a full stop at the end.

Making your own books is a good way of helping children to understand the different forms books can take. They might be simply stapled or sewn down the left side. Folded concertina or zigzag books are particularly useful for sequencing events. There are even book with pages of differing size, such as *The Very Hungry Caterpillar,* by Eric Carle, which shows a different ingredient on each page, building up to a fully illustrated page.

An ABC book of favourite foods with children's illustrations or pictures cut from magazines is another way of teaching about the alphabet. Encourage sorting and classifying by using a variety of pictures of the same item, 'I for ice cream' could show lollies, cones, tubs, and so on.

# Mathematical Development

**Mathematical development is about understanding pattern, sequencing, sorting, matching and counting. It includes working with shape, space, size and measurement.**

You can't do cooking without using mathematics. It involves measuring (quantity, mass and time) as well as counting and sequencing actions. Because it is a practical and enjoyable activity it offers plenty of opportunities for developing mathematical language and problem solving. Laying the table for the correct number of people, lining a circular cake tin, working out how to catch the yolk while separating an egg and how to drain a tin of tomatoes can all be part of the activity, with you posing the problems and asking the all-important questions.

## Numbers and counting

All the recipes contain some numbers. Sometimes these will be small numbers - one teaspoon of lemon juice, two eggs, four carrots - which many children will be able to recognise and read. But there will be higher numbers, too. Naturally there will be numbers on the weights or scales and because the measurements are in grams (only metric weights are taught in schools) many of the numbers you will be using will be large. Most children will not be able to read these but they might be able to identify single digits which make up the number, for instance the 5 in 350. They may also have a growing understanding of large numbers in other contexts, for instance their house number may be 130, they may catch a 75 bus or know that their grandad is 55 years old. So don't be afraid to talk about large numbers and point them out to older children.

## Comparing

Using comparative language when cooking and eating is easy to do - more flour than salt, less butter than milk, more carrots than courgettes, fewer onions than radishes. (Use 'fewer' with objects that can be counted one by one, 'less' with qualities or quantities that cannot be individually counted.) The concept of 'more' is acquired more easily than 'less' so focus on identifying the largest quantities. You will be able to make comparisons with utensils, too: the biggest and smallest spoons, the big bowl and small bowl.

## Adding and subtracting

This is best done in practical activities while you are working with children or when they can see their finished product. 'We have made three jam tarts. How many more do we need to make so that there is one for everybody?' 'If we make one more for Mrs Brown, how many will we have?' 'If the Knave of Hearts took one away, how many would be left?' 'Three carrots and two onions - how many vegetables altogether?'

Very young children may be able to recite numbers in sequence but counting involves an understanding of number. Giving each item a number name as you count it is called one-to-one correspondence and it helps if, at first, children count objects which can be physically moved or touched. They say the number as they move an object from one space to another.

## Fractions

Yes, you really can begin to teach young children fractions! Quarter of a teaspoon of mixed spice or half a lemon may well feature in a recipe but there will be other opportunities too, such as cutting sandwiches in halves or quarters.

## Shape

Shapes can be explored by using cutters and baking tins of different shapes. Help children to make the link between the shape of the container and the shape of the finished article, for example a round cake from a round tin and a square cake from a square tin. Flapjacks or other tray bakes can be sliced into squares, rectangles or triangles.

As you use utensils, look for patterns and shapes that can be identified - the slots in a potato masher, the holes in a garlic press, the cylindrical shape of a rolling pin, the rectangular shape of a chopping board.

Change two-dimensional shapes into three-dimensional ones, for example by rolling rectangular food such as soft, pliable bread spread with cream cheese into cylindrical roly-poly sandwiches. These can be sliced to a more convenient individual size.

## Patterns

Nature is full of patterns. The concentric circles of a sliced carrot, the seeds and flesh in a cut tomato, the gills in an upturned mushroom, the wonder of ice crystals in a partly formed lolly are all there to be seen as are made patterns such as those found in shaped pasta, the tablets in a bar of chocolate or the cubes in a block of jelly. Children can make their own patterns by decorating their food, from iced biscuits to pizza toppings.

## Positional language

Positional language will be used naturally as you work together: 'Pass the spoon next to the big bowl', 'Look underneath the teacloth', 'Slice on top of the chopping board', 'Fold the flour into the mixture'.

## Measurement

You will be measuring quantities when cooking but you will also need to measure time. Time is a difficult concept for children. The language we use to describe it can sometimes be confusing for them; 'soon' is a good example – what may be soon to us may seem an eternity to a child!

There are a number of ways to help children build up their concepts of time:

■ Experiencing and talking about rates of movement (fast/slow) as in the fast whisking of egg whites and the slow setting of ice lollies;

■ Understanding time intervals and relating them to familiar events and routines: 'Before snack time', 'When you go to school tomorrow,' 'Two days until your birthday party';

■ Anticipating and recalling sequences: 'First we chopped the vegetables and then we ……..'

When you are cooking the likelihood is that you will be keeping an eye on the time, particularly if you are baking or waiting for something to set. This is a good opportunity to use a clock and/or timer so that you can give children an indication of the time interval. Say things such as, 'When the big hand gets to the six on the clock, we will take it out of the oven' or 'The icing will take one hour to set so we will set the timer to ring in one hour'. If you have a traditional sand timer, use that too. Whisking for two minutes, kneading bread for five minutes will help children to gain an understanding of short intervals of time.

Seasonal cooking helps children to understand the rhythms of the year - warming soups in winter, mince pies at Christmas, fresh fruit salads in summer. Don't forget to include festival foods for a variety of cultures.

# Knowledge and Understanding of the World

This area of learning covers the skills and attitudes that help children to be curious and to make sense of the world around them.

The concepts and capabilities that children develop in their early years are the building blocks for the science, technology, history and geography that they will study in school. Many changes have happened because people have been curious or have tried to find a new or better way of doing something. They raised the question, looked for an answer and solved a problem.

## Scientific discoveries

It is essential for children to have hands-on opportunities to explore and experiment through planned activities and in their own play. Cookery needs careful supervision but children can still enjoy exploring the materials and ingredients that you use. Build in plenty of time to taste the difference between sugar and salt, feel the flour filtering through fingers, watch the yeast froth, and smell spices as they are warmed in the oven.

Allow children to find out some things for themselves. A little too much water added to a saltdough recipe is not going to do too much harm, and can provide a good learning experience in cause and effect. You can always add more flour later to get it to the right consistency and in sharing this with children you are helping them to develop problem-solving strategies.

Being able to make predictions is a useful life skill but particularly in science, so ask questions such as 'What do you think might happen when we add …….? ' And for older children: 'Why do you think that?'

It is important that children are encouraged to have a go and not to be worried about being right or wrong. They will take their cues from you, so if their prediction did not happen, saying something along the lines of 'Oh, that's interesting, something else has happened, I wonder why that is?' will help them to continue to be curious and not leave them with the feeling that they have made a mistake. Children who develop a strong sense that their predictions are incorrect may be reluctant to offer their ideas in the future. It is worth remembering that there may be several answers to the same question.

As children build up their experience of cooking you will be able to help them to remember and build on past experiences so that they can begin to give a tentative explanation or hypothesis. Such questions as 'You remember when we made cakes and added flour? So what do you think might happen when we add semolina to …….?'

Technological understanding is linked to science. Cookery equipment gives children the chance to pick the tools and techniques they need to shape, assemble and join the materials they are using. Whipping the egg with a fork and choosing the pastry brush to join pastry together and glaze the pie, using a peeler to take the skin off a carrot and a grater to turn the carrot into small pieces are just a few examples. In fact, you cannot do any cooking without technology!

If you have a simple cookery timer or a microwave you will be able to show how programmable equipment works. Tell the children that by pressing certain buttons you programme the machine to tell you when food will be ready.

## Historical links

Every child has their own unique history and personality. They have their own ways of celebrating past and present events and these reflect their family and cultural background. As food is a feature of any celebration throughout the world, there will be many links between food and significant times in their lives.

Celebrations may have their origins in historical events, for example bonfire night, religious festivals such as Passover (Jewish) and Christmas (Christian) or cultural practices relating to a significant event, for example a birthday. Each year also has its pattern of public holidays, national and international events. Because most celebrations are annual they link to the seasons of the year. This may influence the kinds of food used within the celebration. For instance, harvest festival in Britain will include the foods available during late summer and autumn.

Celebrating a birthday by having a party and a cake with candles is a good example of a cultural practice. These events mark the passage of time and may be remembered by children as 'When I was three (or four)'. Memories are often supported and reinforced by photographs, which can be useful in helping children to talk about significant events.

The Christian festivals of Easter and Christmas are associated with chocolate eggs and turkey and Christmas pudding. Over time, some celebrations of religious origin may have lost some of their religious significance but become part of the practices of the particular culture, such as Pancake Day and Hallowe'en. They, too, have

## Scientific words

Cookery involves a great deal of science and although you need not get too involved in the theory there are some scientific principles and vocabulary that it is helpful to know about and try to get right. Children should be encouraged to use the correct words from as early an age as possible.

### Freeze

Freezing is when cold acts upon a substance causing it to change from a liquid into a solid, for example water into ice cubes.

### Melt

Melting is when heat acts upon a substance causing it to change from a solid to a liquid, for example ice lollies to juice, chocolate to chocolate sauce or a runny mess! (Children, and some adults, may incorrectly describe this process as dissolving.)

### Dissolve

Dissolving is when a substance passes into solution or becomes fluid, such as salt in water or sugar in tea.

### Absorb

This is the process by which a solid takes up a liquid, for example beans soaked in water overnight, porridge oats with a little water or raisins soaked before making a fruit cake.

### Evaporate

When a liquid turns into a vapour. You can see this happening when you boil water or soup and the steam (vapour) rises out of the saucepan into the air above. If you go on boiling for too long, all the liquid will evaporate and disappear.

### Settle

Settlement takes place when the larger and heavier particles in a mixture settle to the bottom, leaving a liquid at the top. You can see this in pureed apple and some soups, such as leek and potato. (You can show it more clearly when soil particles are mixed vigorously in a jar of water. For the best results use a mixture containing gravel, sand, and soil and allow half an hour for settlement to take place.)

### Reversible and irreversible change

Reversible change is when ice melts into water, because it may be reversed and refrozen into ice. Chocolate may be treated the same way.

A cake mix once made into a cake is permanent. A cooked cake cannot be turned back into a cake mix and therefore the change that heat makes in this instance is irreversible.

particular foods associated with them. Your approach to religious festivals should be sensitive to the religious background of the children and their families and to the context of your own home or setting. Find out plenty about festivals by talking to families and knowledgeable members in the community.

## A sense of time

Children need some routines in their day. It helps them to anticipate what comes next and gives them a sense of order and security. A regular snack time during the morning not only provides nourishment and an opportunity to share a social event but also helps children to sequence events in the day and gives a sense of pattern in the passing of time.

## A sense of place

Food is bound to have some relevance within your local environment. If you live and work in a rural area then the chances are that food grows or lives around you - from the barley growing in the field to the milk from the cows! In urban areas there is likely to be anything from a garage or corner shop selling bare essentials to a large parade of shops or a supermarket.

In helping children to identify features in the place they live you will be locating places where food is grown or bought. The best way to do this is to take a walk, with a camera if possible. Pictures of food outlets, perhaps a shop or the local allotments, can be used to help prompt memories and to identify features not noticed on the walk.

As travel becomes easier and cheaper, a greater number of children have experience of faraway places. They may have been on holiday abroad and eaten foods from different countries and met people from different cultural backgrounds. They may have returned to the country where their grandparents were born and tasted similar foods but in a different context. These experiences can be shared through talk and photographs and recorded and reinterpreted through drawing and model making.

**TEACHING POINTS**

If all the children cannot experience a cooking session on a given day then setting up a rota and knowing when it will be their turn gives children a sense of order and fairness.

When looking at the ingredients for a recipe it may be appropriate to talk about where the food comes from. The shop, of course - but how does it get to the shop?

Through television and their own travel, some older children may have an awareness of other countries, where weather and food may be different. For these children you might talk about the countries where some of the food comes from; fruits such as grapes and oranges are easy to start with as children who have visited Mediterranean countries may well have seen them growing. Although it will be some time before young children fully understand that the world may be represented by a map or globe, you can certainly use them to begin to develop that global awareness.

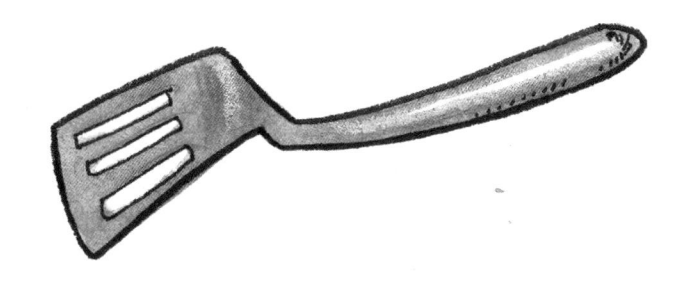

# Physical Development

**Cookery involves using your hands and requires you to control and coordinate tools, equipment and materials.**

Children learn best by doing and not just watching, so show them how to use the tools, explain carefully what you are doing and why and then pass the tools to them.

While children are waiting for their turn, ask others to watch how carefully 'Sam is sieving the flour by keeping the sieve over the bowl and not shaking too hard... ' or 'Charlotte is grating the cheese but her fingers are not near the cutting edge...' By describing the action in a positive way you are sensitively reinforcing safety rules, helping those waiting to be observant and preparing them for their turn. You will also be building the confidence of the child who is doing the action.

Be careful not to leap in too quickly to help children with the more tricky but safe bits; you could be denying them some of the richest experiences. So when stirring flour into a cake mix let them all experience the physical sensation of the thickening mixture and let them find out how their arm aches! This helps them to recognise the changes that happen in their body when they are active. And they will have a greater sense of achievement at the end of the process if they have been challenged a little bit, too.

Safety is really important in cooking. Children should be expected to use the tools carefully and to respect your warnings.

# Creative Development

**Cooking is a creative activity that provides the chance to explore texture, colour, shape and form.**

### Texture

We live in a world of pre-packaged, frozen and fast food. The opportunities for snapping fresh peas from the pod or feeling the gritty earth on a potato are fast disappearing. That's why it is all the more important for children to handle raw ingredients and be able to respond to their sense of touch.

Allow plenty of time for children to feel and compare raw ingredients. If you are worried about children touching the food, set up a few small bowls of ingredients just for the purpose of exploring their textures and scents.

Texture does not always have to be experienced by direct touch. Children will feel the differences in stirring a bowl when different ingredients are added. They will experience:

- the sloppiness of a cake mixture when egg is added;
- the slipperiness of a hard-boiled egg as they try to cut it;
- the crunch of biscuits being rolled into pieces.

Help them to find the words to express their feelings and ideas and be ready to supply descriptive words for them.

## Colour

Making food look appetising is all part of the skill of being a cook.

Professional cooks often use colour imaginatively to improve the look of a dish and to express their creative flair. Young children, too, can use their imagination in making food look attractive. Using off-cuts of pastry is an ideal way to add decoration to pies. They could try cutting the initial letter of their name.

There is a wide range of decorating ingredients which children can use to individualise their small buns and cakes. Pizzas make an excellent palette for colour and can be decorated with all their favourite ingredients.

Soups and salads can be decorated with chopped herbs and sweet dishes decorated with sliced fresh fruit.

When you prepare fruit or vegetables for snacks, think about how you arrange the different coloured food on the plate. Try not to put bland colours together but intersperse them with brighter coloured food. For example, place white celery next to carrot sticks followed by sliced apple. Draw children's attention to the coloured pattern you make.

## Shape and form

Cutting and slicing are ideal ways in which food can be prepared and shaped to make them attractive. There are many links that can be made with children's learning of mathematical shapes. Try to show different ways of cutting the same ingredient. A carrot cut horizontally makes circles; sliced vertically it makes sticks.

Bread making gives rich opportunities to explore form in a three-dimensional way. Children will delight in being able to push, pull and roll the soft, pliable dough into different shapes.

Pastry gives children many ways of creating irregular random shapes. These can be pieced together to make abstract and edible pictures.

## Being creative with food

Food, particularly pasta because of its diverse shapes and colours, is often used for collage picture making.

Raw and cooked food may be used in a number of ways to offer children sensory experiences. There is something wonderfully soothing about scooping up handfuls of rice and allowing it to trickle through the fingers. Any dried grain or pulse may be used in this way. Place it in a large open plastic box and keep a dustpan and brush close by!

Cooked pasta mixed with a liquid poster paint can give another kind of experience. A blue paint would be ideal as there are not many blue foods that we eat and therefore the children are less likely to try and eat it!

## Imaginative play

Play areas provide social settings that help children make sense of the world around them. They allow children to reconstruct their experiences without a sense of failure.

- Restaurants – from seaside cafes, fish and chip shops to Chinese restaurants and Indian take-aways
- Shops – from supermarkets to the local corner shop, greengrocers/ farm shop and baker's
- Kitchen/home corner with cooking facilities
- Garage with shopping facilities (this would be ideal for the garden where trikes and bikes could be used)
- Ice-cream parlour / van
- Small world play – farms

When you set up a play area it is always best, if possible, for children to have the real experience first, either with their families or their early years setting. Then they will be able to contribute their own ideas for the toys or resources that they need.

Drama can play a part in helping children to develop confidence as well as speaking and listening skills. There are many stories in which food plays a part, for example 'The Gingerbread Man' and 'Goldilocks and the Three Bears', which can be re-enacted. You will need to prompt and remind the children as they re-play the stories. Keep props simple and the whole activity should be quick and fun. Everyone can join in with phrases such as: 'Run run as fast as you can, You can't catch me I'm the Gingerbread Man.'

There are many traditional poems and action rhymes which refer to food. You will find some in the activities alongside the recipes in this book. Why not make a list of the ones you know already, starting with that well-known egg, Humpty Dumpty?

## Music from food

Simple shakers can be made using a plastic bottle or two similar plastic containers, such as yoghurt pots, stuck together. Fill each container with a different kind of dried pulse or grain. Make sure the food is sufficiently different in size so that you get a range of sounds from the finished instruments.

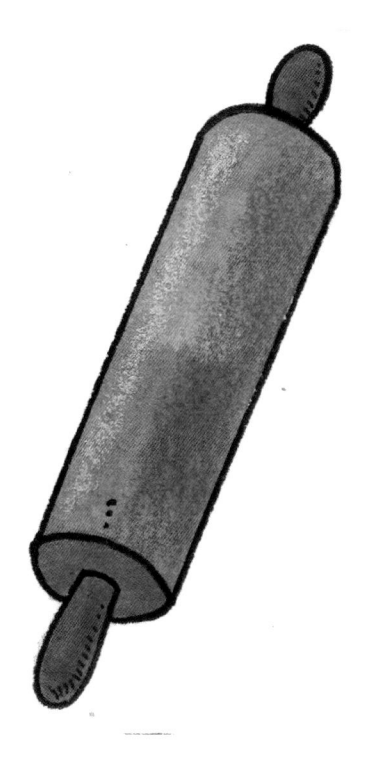

### TEACHING POINTS

Children who are unable to use tools carefully on their own in a group situation should have another adult to work alongside them so they can still be included.

**Please note:**
Be aware that some people are sensitive to the use of food for anything other than eating. Their view is that food should be respected as a life giving force and should not be used for trivial purposes. No-one would wish to offend colleagues or parents in this way and their views and opinions should be respected.

# Health and safety

## Allergies
Before you start a cookery session it is important to know whether any children have allergies to certain foods, such as nuts. If you're in any doubt, check with their parents and be vigilant if you know that it's the first time a child has tried a certain ingredient. If you work with children, keep records of any allergies or dietary requirements.

## Multicultural considerations
Some cultures have additional hygiene practices and you may be cooking with children who have been brought up to respect them. You need to make sure that you are aware of this. In some cultures, for example, only the right hand is used to eat with and it is washed with special care. Some faiths have particular dietary customs. It is well known that meat has strong religious traditions but eggs, animal products such as milk, cheese and fats as well as stimulants such as cocoa, tea and coffee may also be taboo. It is important to know about the faiths and cultural background of children and their dietary customs.

## Supervision
If you're cooking with a group of children, the smaller the group the better. Four children to one adult is manageable. Having a small group makes it easier for everyone to be closely involved and there's not too much waiting for a turn. Never leave children unsupervised in a kitchen.

## Food hygiene
Keeping bad bugs out of food is important. Common causes for the spread of food born illness include: not cooking food right through, not washing and re-washing hands, dirty equipment, especially dish cloths, and leaving food uncovered in warm temperatures for too long.

Make sure all work surfaces and chopping boards are clean at the start of the session and scrub them again at the end.

Children need to wash their hands thoroughly, especially between the fingers, with soap and warm water. Show them how to interweave the fingers of one hand with those of the other so that the soap can get into all the crevices. Give children a novelty soap to encourage them with this chore.

Make sure that any cuts or grazes are well covered with waterproof dressings.

Long hair should be tied back and sleeves rolled up. Clean aprons, used just for cookery, should be worn.

When food is left to cool, cover it with a clean tea towel and wrap as soon as it is cool.

Sampling and tasting is one way in which a cook makes sure that flavours are well adjusted and, of course, children love licking spoons, but care needs to be taken if the

## Safety rules
Common sense rules need to be emphasised with young children.

■ Don't allow a young child to put food in or out of the oven.

■ Turn the handles of saucepans away, especially when they are on the cooker, to prevent them from being caught and tipped by small hands.

■ Leave food to cool to a comfortable heat before being sampled.

■ Extra care may need to be taken if children are using glass. Wherever possible use toughened glass (for example, Pyrex).

■ Children should be taught to use knives properly and safely. They don't need a razor sharp knife but they do need one that is good enough to cut up vegetables and fruit. A blunt knife can be dangerous because children get frustrated and may apply too much pressure.

■ If you need a sharper knife or implement keep it well out of children's reach.

■ Watch children carefully when they are using a grater – it is easy to grate a finger!

recipe contains raw egg. There may be a risk of salmonella and therefore tasting should be avoided. Explain that some uncooked foods can cause stomach ache.

## Storage

Remember to use all kinds of food within the 'best before' or 'use by' dates. Weevils may appear in flour or other grains if kept for too long.

Buy whole spices where you can as ground spices lose their colour and smell quickly and, of course, they are a source of interest to children.

Make sure all utensils are dry before storing. If you're in a school or nursery, a cupboard kept for cooking and baking utensils is ideal, otherwise use a plastic storage box with a lid.

## Fridge storage

Be sure that the fridge is kept cold enough - between 1°C and 5°C. Keep the door closed and open it as few times as possible. Don't warm up the fridge by putting warm food in it. Let the food cool down first. Buy a fridge thermometer and place it near the front of a top shelf and check it regularly.

Store raw food on the bottom shelves.

De-frost regularly and wash out using a little bicarbonate of soda in water or mild disinfectant.

## Tidying up

Some spills and mess are inevitable when cooking with children but they need to be cleared up promptly, particularly if they involve water on the floor, which could cause someone to slip.

Always encourage children to help clear away. It will be another chance to get across health and hygiene messages as well as for children to show responsibility and care for the equipment. Most young children also think it's fun!

Provide a bowl of warm water and cloths to wipe down work surfaces and a dust pan and brush, plus a separate cloth for the floor.

Help children to do as much of the washing and wiping up as possible, taking special care where sharp tools or glass have been used. If they can't reach the sink, take bowls of washing-up water to the work area.

### TEACHING POINTS

A food hygiene course will provide a good grounding in personal hygiene, care of equipment, how to prepare and store food safely and help identify high-risk foods. Most local councils offer a day course. Further information is available from:

The Support Centre Team and Training Division, Charted Institute of Environmental Health, Chadwick Court, 15 Hatfields, London SE1 8DJ.
Tel: 0207 9286006
www.cieh.org.uk